Personal Liberty

Other Books in the Issues on Trial Series:

Personal Liberty

Uma Kukathas, Book Editor

GREENHAVEN PRESS
A part of Gale, Cengage Learning

Detroit • New York • San Francisco • New Haven, Conn • Waterville, Maine • London

Christine Nasso, *Publisher*
Elizabeth Des Chenes, *Managing Editor*

© 2009 Greenhaven Press, a part of Gale, Cengage Learning

For more information, contact:
Greenhaven Press
27500 Drake Rd.
Farmington Hills, MI 48331-3535
Or you can visit our Internet site at gale.cengage.com.

For product information and technology assistance, contact us at

Gale Customer Support, 1-800-877-4253
For permission to use material from this text or product, submit all requests online at www.cengage.com/permissions

Further permissions questions can be emailed to permissionrequest@cengage.com

Articles in Greenhaven Press anthologies are often edited for length to meet page requirements. In addition, original titles of these works are changed to clearly present the main thesis and to explicitly indicate the author's opinion. Every effort is made to ensure that Greenhaven Press accurately reflects the original intent of the authors. Every effort has been made to trace the owners of copyrighted material.

Cover photograph reproduced by permission of Karen Bleier/AFP/Getty Images.

LIBRARY OF CONGRESS CATALOGING-IN-PUBLICATION DATA

Personal liberty / Uma Kukathas, book editor.
    p. cm. -- (Issues on trial)
    Includes bibliographical references and index.
    ISBN-13: 978-0-7377-4343-2 (hardcover)
    1. Civil rights--United States. I. Kukathas, Uma.
    KF4749.P434 2009
    342.7308'5--dc22

                                                            2009005235

Printed in the United States of America
1 2 3 4 5 6 7 13 12 11 10 09

Contents

Chapter 2: Declaring Interracial Marriage Restrictions Unconstitutional

Chapter 3: Refusing the Freedom to Die

Chapter 4: Allowing Sexual Liberty Between Consenting Adults

Foreword

The U.S. courts have long served as a battleground for the most highly charged and contentious issues of the time. Divisive matters are often brought into the legal system by activists who feel strongly for their cause and demand an official resolution. Indeed, subjects that give rise to intense emotions or involve closely held religious or moral beliefs lay at the heart of the most polemical court rulings in history. One such case was *Brown v. Board of Education* (1954), which ended racial segregation in schools. Prior to *Brown*, the courts had held that blacks could be forced to use separate facilities as long as these facilities were equal to that of whites.

For years many groups had opposed segregation based on religious, moral, and legal grounds. Educators produced heartfelt testimony that segregated schooling greatly disadvantaged black children. They noted that in comparison to whites, blacks received a substandard education in deplorable conditions. Religious leaders such as Martin Luther King Jr. preached that the harsh treatment of blacks was immoral and unjust. Many involved in civil rights law, such as Thurgood Marshall, called for equal protection of all people under the law, as their study of the Constitution had indicated that segregation was illegal and un-American. Whatever their motivation for ending the practice, and despite the threats they received from segregationists, these ardent activists remained unwavering in their cause.

Those fighting against the integration of schools were mainly white southerners who did not believe that whites and blacks should intermingle. Blacks were subordinate to whites, they maintained, and society had to resist any attempt to break down strict color lines. Some white southerners charged that segregated schooling was *not* hindering blacks' education. For example, Virginia attorney general J. Lindsay Almond asserted, "With the help and the sympathy and the love and respect of the white people of the South, the colored man has risen under that educational process to a place of eminence and respect throughout the nation. It has served him well." So when the Supreme Court ruled against the segregationists in *Brown*, the South responded with vociferous cries of protest. Even government leaders criticized the decision. The governor of Arkansas, Orval Faubus, stated that he would not "be a party to any attempt to force acceptance of change to which the people are so overwhelmingly opposed." Indeed, resistance to integration was so great that when black students arrived at the formerly all-white Central High School in Arkansas, federal troops had to be dispatched to quell a threatening mob of protesters.

Nevertheless, the *Brown* decision was enforced and the South integrated its schools. In this instance, the Court, while not settling the issue to everyone's satisfaction, functioned as an instrument of progress by forcing a major social change. Historian David Halberstam observes that the *Brown* ruling "deprived segregationist practices of their moral legitimacy. . . . It was therefore perhaps the single most important moment of the decade, the moment that separated the old order from the new and helped create the tumultuous era just arriving." Considered one of the most important victories for civil rights, *Brown* paved the way for challenges to racial segregation in many areas, including on public buses and in restaurants.

In examining *Brown*, it becomes apparent that the courts play an influential role—and face an arduous challenge—in shaping the debate over emotionally charged social issues. Judges must balance competing interests, keeping in mind the high stakes and intense emotions on both sides. As exemplified by *Brown*, judicial decisions often upset the status quo and initiate significant changes in society. Greenhaven Press's Issues on Trial series captures the controversy surrounding influential court rulings and explores the social ramifications of such decisions from varying perspectives. Each anthology highlights one social issue—such as the death penalty, students' rights, or wartime civil liberties. Each volume then focuses on key historical and contemporary court cases that helped mold the issue as we know it today. The books include a compendium of primary sources—court rulings, dissents, and immediate reactions to the rulings—as well as secondary sources from experts in the field, people involved in the cases, legal analysts, and other commentators opining on the implications and legacy of the chosen cases. An annotated table of contents, an in-depth introduction, and prefaces that overview each case all provide context as readers delve into the topic at hand. To help students fully probe the subject, each volume contains book and periodical bibliographies, a comprehensive index, and a list of organizations to contact. With these features, the Issues on Trial series offers a well-rounded perspective on the courts' role in framing society's thorniest, most impassioned debates.

Introduction

The notion of personal liberty is abstract and difficult to define, but it is also the foundation of American democracy. Personal liberty is the ideal that is articulated in the Declaration of Independence when it states that all persons, being equal, are entitled to "life, liberty, and the pursuit of happiness." The authors of the declaration regarded personal liberty as intrinsic to the human condition. As they went on to say in that famous document, governments and constitutions exist in order to secure this and other freedoms.

Personal liberty is often regarded as synonymous with "civil liberty," which is a freedom that protects the individual from the government, such as freedom of religion, freedom of speech, and additionally, the right to due process, to a fair trial, to own property, and to privacy. There is vigorous debate regarding exactly what constitutes a personal liberty. For example, while few dispute the idea that marriage is a fundamental personal liberty, it is not so clear to everyone that reproductive rights or the right to marry someone of the same sex are "freedoms" that ought to be guaranteed by law. Personal liberty is a freedom that protects individuals from undue governmental interference in their lives, but it is acknowledged also that there is a need to balance public welfare against individual liberties, so some personal freedoms must be restricted for the common good and public order.

In American legal history, cases involving personal liberty have most often referenced the Fourteenth Amendment. When individuals have brought suit against states, they have claimed that their Fourteenth Amendment rights to "due process" or to "equal protection" have been violated by unfair state laws. They have argued that the state law has interfered with or denied them certain fundamental rights. States defending or bringing suits against individuals have claimed that their laws do not violate the Fourteenth Amendment, are constitutional, and should have legal binding force.

The Bill of Rights, the first ten amendments to the United States Constitution, prohibits the government from depriving any person of "life, liberty, or property, without due process of law." However, before 1868, the Bill of Rights applied only to the federal government and not to the states. The ratification of the Fourteenth Amendment after the Civil War provided that individual states, and not just the national government, may not deprive any person of life, liberty, or property without "due process of law." Written originally to protect former slaves, the Fourteenth Amendment further guarantees every American the right to equal protection and the right to the privileges and immunities of national citizenship.

The due process clause of the Fourteenth Amendment imposes certain procedural requirements on governments when they interfere with life, liberty, or property. For more than half a century after the amendment was ratified, the Supreme Court took this to mean that the protection of civil liberties was to be left to state law; it was up to states to ensure citizens were not deprived of their rights. Numerous cases that came before the Court claiming that the amendment should require state governments to respect the guarantees of the Bill of Rights were dismissed. However, in a series of decisions beginning in the early twentieth century, the Supreme Court read the Fourteenth Amendment's liberty clause as prohibiting states from interfering with the private decisions and conduct of individuals. The due process clause came to be understood by the Supreme Court as limiting the substantive power of the states to regulate certain areas of human life; government may not so interfere with citizens' "fundamental" rights that they amount to an unconstitutional denial of "liberty." "Substantive due process," as it has come to be understood, protects certain fundamental rights and liberty interests no matter the procedure used to deprive a person of that liberty. Laws must be related to a legitimate government interest (e.g., crime prevention) and not contain provisions that result in the unfair or arbitrary treatment of an individual.

Beginning in the early twentieth century, the Supreme Court began to selectively incorporate some of the specific provisions of the Bill of Rights with the idea that certain provisions "fundamental to the American scheme of justice" in it are made applicable to the states by the due process clause. In *Gitlow v. New York* (1925), the Court held that the First Amendment protection of freedom of speech applied to the states through the due process clause. In *Palko v. Connecticut* (1937), the Court decided that some privileges and immunities of the Bill of Rights were so fundamental that states must abide by them through the due process clause. By the late 1940s, many civil freedoms, including freedom of the press, had been incorporated, as had many rights applying to defendants in criminal cases. In 1947, Justice Hugo Black argued that the Fourteenth Amendment incorporated all aspects of the Bill of Rights and applied them to the states, and after 1962, most provisions of the Bill of Rights were eventually incorporated to apply to the states.

In 1965 a Fourteenth Amendment case was heard that has had an enormous impact on the idea of personal liberty in American jurisprudence. Beginning as early as 1923, the Court had hinted that the "liberty" guarantee of the Fourteenth Amendment guaranteed a right of privacy. In *Meyer v. Nebraska* (1923), the Court struck down a state law prohibiting teachers and parents from educating their children in the manner and language of their choosing. In his written opinion, Justice James Clark McReynolds wrote, "The Court has never attempted with much exactness to define liberty. Without doubt, it denotes not merely the freedom from bodily restraint but also the right of the individual to contract, to engage in any of the common occupations of life, to acquire useful knowledge, to worship according to the dictates of their own conscience, to marry, establish a home, bring up children, and generally to enjoy those privileges long recognized at common law as essential to the orderly pursuit of happiness." Forty-two years later, this notion of protected personal liberty was taken up in the landmark *Griswold v. Connecticut* decision, which specified that the Bill of Rights did in fact contain a general "right to privacy." In that case, the Court held that Connecticut's anti-contraceptive law (making it a crime for anyone to give out information or instructions on the use of birth control devices) intruded upon notions of privacy surrounding the ideas of marital privilege and reproductive rights. This notion that there is a "generalized right to privacy" was used in deciding *Roe v. Wade* (1973), which holds that a woman's right to privacy allows her to have an abortion if she chooses.

In a series of other rulings, the Court has held that the due process clause of the Fourteenth Amendment protects other important personal liberties. In *Loving v. Virginia* (1967), the Court held that marriage is a fundamental right and that there is no compelling interest for the state to prevent people of different races from getting married. The Court affirmed the personal liberty of gays and lesbians in its 2003 decision in *Lawrence v. Texas* (2003), which overturned a Texas statute criminalizing certain sexual acts between same-sex couples. However, the Court has concluded that the due process clause does not protect all personal liberties, as seen in the 1997 decision of *Washington v. Glucksberg*, in which a unanimous Court agreed there is no fundamental right to committing suicide with the aid of a physician. But, as Justice William Rehnquist noted in his opinion in that case, the debate on the issue will and should go on. Indeed it is the great strength of American democracy that this and other controversial questions surrounding personal liberty continue to be the subject of serious discussion and legal deliberation.

CHAPTER 1

Embracing the Right to Privacy

Case Overview

Griswold v. Connecticut (1965)

In 1879, the state of Connecticut enacted a law banning the sale and use of contraceptives. The law further criminalized anyone who counseled others in the use of birth control. Originally written by the legislator P.T. Barnum, chairman of the House Committee on Temperance and the former circus showman, the law was controversial, unpopular, and seldom enforced. But it remained on the books, withstanding more than eighty years of legislative and legal challenges. In November 1961, the statute was again challenged, this time by two people who had been fighting unsuccessfully for years to overturn the law. Estelle Griswold, executive director of the Planned Parenthood League of Connecticut (PPLC) and her colleague, Lee Buxton, a physician and professor at Yale Medical School, decided to break the law themselves by opening a clinic offering family planning counseling and birth control to married couples. For their violation of the 1879 law, they were arrested, convicted, and fined $100 each.

Griswold and Buxton appealed, and their case rose through the state courts all the way to the Connecticut Supreme Court, but their convictions were upheld. They took their case to the United States Supreme Court, where a noted First Amendment scholar, Thomas I. Emerson, argued that the Connecticut statute deprived his clients and their patients of the First Amendment right to free speech and their right to liberty, which according to the Fourteenth Amendment they could not be deprived of without "due process of law." Emerson further claimed that Griswold and Buxton had a right to privacy guaranteed by the Ninth Amendment, and that the state was misdirected in upholding a law that sought to legislate a morality not consistent with the standards of the community.

In a 7-2 decision written by Justice William O. Douglas, the Court ruled that the Connecticut anti-contraceptive law violated the "right to marital privacy" and could not be enforced against married couples. In what is viewed as one of the Court's most controversial opinions, Justice Douglas contended that the Bill of Rights' specific guarantees have "penumbras," or shadowy areas, that are created by "emanations from these guarantees that help give them life and opinion." That is, there is a general "right to privacy" implied in the Constitution: the First, Third, Fourth, Fifth, and Ninth Amendments contain liberties that, when applied against the states by the Fourteenth Amendment, create a "right to privacy" that cannot be unjustifiably infringed. This right is "fundamental" when it comes to the actions of married couples, because to deny it would be to violate basic principles of liberty and justice that are the foundation of American civil and political institutions. Connecticut, said the Court, had no compelling reason to overcome this fundamental right, hence the 1879 law was unconstitutional. In his dissent, Justice Hugo Black condemned the decision as stretching judicial authority, finding it preposterous that the majority claimed to have "discovered" such a right to privacy in the Constitution and seeing it as dangerous to allow the federal government to make a legislative decision that should be left to the state of Connecticut.

In *Griswold* the Supreme Court recognized a specific constitutional right to privacy in matters of marital intimacy and reproduction, but it opened the door to establishing a basic sphere of personal privacy to which all people are entitled. This right is one of the most disputed in American jurisprudence. As a precedent, *Griswold* has had enormous impact, particularly because it paved the way for *Roe v. Wade* (1973), which held that a woman's privacy included a right to choose whether or not her pregnancy should be terminated. *Griswold* has functioned as the legal basis for judicial rulings involving sexual intimacy, reproductive rights, and family life. It remains central in debates about privacy and questions about how the Constitution should be interpreted.

> *"The present case, then, concerns a rela-*
> *tionship lying within the zone of pri-*
> *vacy created by several fundamental*
> *constitutional guarantees."*

The Court's Decision: The Right of Privacy Is a Fundamental Right

William O. Douglas

William O. Douglas, who was nominated to the Supreme Court by President Franklin D. Roosevelt in 1939, served on the bench for more than thirty-six years. He was considered an individual-ist who held the view that the law should be expanded in order to protect individual rights. In his opinion in the case of Gris-wold v. Connecticut, Justice Douglas argues that a right to pri-vacy is to be found within the Constitution, even if it is not stated explicitly. Thus, the conviction of two persons under a Connecticut law that prohibits the use of drugs or other instru-ments to prevent conception, and providing assistance or counsel in their use, violated their constitutional rights. Estelle Griswold and Dr. C. Lee Buxton, who operated a birth control clinic, had been convicted as accessories for providing married couples with information and medical advice on how to prevent conception and for prescribing contraceptive devices and materials. The Court ruled against Connecticut, asserting that its legal statute forbidding use of contraceptives "violates the right of marital privacy which is within the penumbra of specific guarantees of the Bill of Rights." According to Douglas, people have more

William O. Douglas, majority opinion, *Griswold v. Connecticut*, U.S. Supreme Court, June 7, 1965.

rights that can be read in the literal language of the Constitution, and privacy is one of them. Douglas asserts that the Griswold case concerns a relationship that lies within the zone of privacy that is created by constitutional guarantees, and thus the law that seeks to invade it cannot stand.

Appellant Griswold is Executive Director of the Planned Parenthood League of Connecticut. Appellant Buxton is a licensed physician and a professor at the Yale Medical School who served as Medical Director for the League at its Center in New Haven—a center open and operating from November 1 to November 10, 1961, when appellants were arrested.

They gave information, instruction, and medical advice to *married persons* as to the means of preventing conception. They examined the wife and prescribed the best contraceptive device or material for her use. Fees were usually charged, although some couples were serviced free.

Connecticut Statutes Involved in This Case

The statutes whose constitutionality is involved in this appeal are §§53-32 and 54-196 of the General Statutes of Connecticut. The former provides:

> Any person who uses any drug, medicinal article or instrument for the purpose of preventing conception shall be fined not less than fifty dollars or imprisoned not less than sixty days nor more than one year or be both fined and imprisoned.

Section 54-196 provides:

> Any person who assists, abets, counsels, causes, hires or commands another to commit any offense may be prosecuted and punished as if he were the principal offender.

The appellants were found guilty as accessories and fined $100 each, against the claim that the accessory statute, as so applied, violated the Fourteenth Amendment. The Appellate Division of the Circuit Court affirmed. The Supreme Court of Errors affirmed that judgment. We noted probable jurisdiction.

Constitutional Rights of the Married Clients

We think that appellants have standing to raise the constitutional rights of the married people with whom they had a professional relationship. *Tileston v. Ullman,* is different, for there the plaintiff seeking to represent others asked for a declaratory Judgment. In that situation, we thought that the requirements of standing should be strict, lest the standards of "case or controversy" in Article III of the Constitution become blurred. Here, those doubts are removed by reason of a criminal conviction for serving married couples in violation of an aiding-and-abetting statute. Certainly the accessory should have standing to assert that the offense which he is charged with assisting is not, or cannot constitutionally be, a crime.

This case is more akin to *Truax v. Raich,* where an employee was permitted to assert the rights of his employer; to *Pierce v. Society of Sisters,* where the owners of private schools were entitled to assert the rights of potential pupils and their parents, and to *Barrows v. Jackson,* where a white defendant, party to a racially restrictive covenant, who was being sued for damages by the covenantors because she had conveyed her property to Negroes, was allowed to raise the issue that enforcement of the covenant violated the rights of prospective Negro purchasers to equal protection, although no Negro was a party to the suit. The rights of husband and wife, pressed here, are likely to be diluted or adversely affected unless those rights are considered in a suit involving those who have this kind of confidential relation to them.

Intimate Relations of Married Persons and the Fourteenth Amendment

Coming to the merits, we are met with a wide range of questions that implicate the Due Process Clause of the Fourteenth Amendment. Overtones of some arguments suggest that *Lochner v. New York*, should be our guide. But we decline that invitation, as we did in *West Coast Hotel Co. v. Parrish*, *Olsen v. Nebraska*, *Lincoln Union v. Northwestern Co.*, *Williamson v. Lee Optical Co.*, *Giboney v. Empire Storage Co.* We do not sit as a super-legislature to determine the wisdom, need, and propriety of laws that touch economic problems, business affairs, or social conditions. This law, however, operates directly on an intimate relation of husband and wife and their physician's role in one aspect of that relation.

Rights Not Explicitly Stated in the Constitution and Bill of Rights

The association of people is not mentioned in the Constitution nor in the Bill of Rights. The right to educate a child in a school of the parents' choice—whether public or private or parochial—is also not mentioned. Nor is the right to study any particular subject or any foreign language. Yet the First Amendment has been construed to include certain of those rights.

By *Pierce v. Society of Sisters*, the right to educate one's children as one chooses is made applicable to the States by the force of the First and Fourteenth Amendments. By *Meyer v. Nebraska*, the same dignity is given the right to study the German language in a private school. In other words, the State may not, consistently with the spirit of the First Amendment, contract the spectrum of available knowledge. The right of freedom of speech and press includes not only the right to utter or to print, but the right to distribute, the right to receive, the right to read and freedom of inquiry, freedom of thought, and freedom to teach—indeed, the freedom of the entire university community. Without those peripheral rights, the specific rights would be less secure. And so we reaffirm the principle of the *Pierce* and the *Meyer* cases.

In *NAACP v. Alabama*, we protected the "freedom to associate and privacy in one's associations," noting that freedom of association was a peripheral First Amendment right. Disclosure of membership lists of a constitutionally valid association, we held, was invalid

> as entailing the likelihood of a substantial restraint upon the exercise by petitioner's members of their right to freedom of association.

In other words, the First Amendment has a penumbra where privacy is protected from governmental intrusion. In like context, we have protected forms of "association" that are not political in the customary sense, but pertain to the social, legal, and economic benefit of the members. In *Schware v. Board of Bar Examiners*, we held it not permissible to bar a lawyer from practice because he had once been a member of the Communist Party. The man's "association with that Party" was not shown to be "anything more than a political faith in a political party," and was not action of a kind proving bad moral character.

Those cases involved more than the "right of assembly"—a right that extends to all, irrespective of their race or ideology. The right of "association," like the right of belief, is more than the right to attend a meeting; it includes the right to express one's attitudes or philosophies by membership in a group or by affiliation with it or by other lawful means. Association in that context is a form of expression of opinion, and, while it is not expressly included in the First Amendment, its existence is necessary in making the express guarantees fully meaningful.

Penumbral Rights

The foregoing cases suggest that specific guarantees in the Bill of Rights have penumbras, formed by emanations from those guarantees that help give them life and substance. Various guarantees create zones of privacy. The right of association contained in the penumbra of the First Amendment is one, as we have seen. The Third Amendment, in its prohibition against the quartering of soldiers "in any house" in time of peace without the consent of the owner, is another facet of that privacy. The Fourth Amendment explicitly affirms the "right of the people to be secure in their persons, houses, papers, and effects, against unreasonable searches and seizures." The Fifth Amendment, in its Self-Incrimination Clause, enables the citizen to create a zone of privacy which government may not force him to surrender to his detriment. The Ninth Amendment provides: "The enumeration in the Constitution, of certain rights, shall not be construed to deny or disparage others retained by the people."

The Fourth and Fifth Amendments were described in *Boyd v. United States*, as protection against all governmental invasions "of the sanctity of a man's home and the privacies of life." We recently referred in *Mapp v. Ohio*, to the Fourth Amendment as creating a "right to privacy, no less important than any other right carefully and particularly reserved to the people."

We have had many controversies over these penumbral rights of "privacy and repose." These cases bear witness that the right of privacy which presses for recognition here is a legitimate one.

Marriage Lies Within the "Zone of Privacy"

The present case, then, concerns a relationship lying within the zone of privacy created by several fundamental constitutional guarantees. And it concerns a law which, in forbidding the use of contraceptives, rather than regulating their manufacture or sale, seeks to achieve its goals by means having a maximum destructive impact upon that relationship. Such a law cannot stand in light of the familiar principle, so often applied by this Court, that a

> governmental purpose to control or prevent activities constitutionally subject to state regulation may not be achieved by means which sweep unnecessarily broadly and thereby invade the area of protected freedoms.

NAACP v. Alabama. Would we allow the police to search the sacred precincts of marital bedrooms for telltale signs of the use of contraceptives? The very idea is repulsive to the notions of privacy surrounding the marriage relationship.

We deal with a right of privacy older than the Bill of Rights—older than our political parties, older than our school system. Marriage is a coming together for better or for worse, hopefully enduring, and intimate to the degree of being sacred. It is an association that promotes a way of life, not causes; a harmony in living, not political faiths; a bilateral loyalty, not commercial or social projects. Yet it is an association for as noble a purpose as any involved in our prior decisions.

"I like my privacy as well as the next one, but I am nevertheless compelled to admit that government has a right to invade it."

Dissenting Opinion: There Is No Right to Privacy Stated in the Constitution

Hugo Black

Hugo Black, who served as a Democratic senator, was President Franklin D. Roosevelt's first appointment to the Supreme Court. In his dissenting opinion in the case of Griswold v. Connecticut, *Black says that although the Connecticut law under which the two appellants were convicted is an offensive one, it is not unconstitutional. In the case, Estelle Griswold and Dr. C. Lee Buxton, who ran a birth control clinic, had been convicted as accessories under an 1879 Connecticut law that made it illegal to use, assist, or counsel anyone to use contraceptives. The Court, in a 7-2 majority, ruled in favor of Griswold and Buxton, citing that the law under which they were convicted violated the constitutional right to privacy. Black argues that the other justices who discovered the supposed right—whether because of their views of "implied rights" or theories or "natural justice"—lacked specific constitutional authorization. He views the decision as a mistaken exercise of their judicial power in a manner that threatens the American system of government. "Use of any such broad, unbounded judicial authority would make of this Court's members a day-to-day constitutional convention," he argues. Any decision to change or abandon the Connecticut law, he says, should*

Hugo Black, dissenting opinion, *Griswold v. Connecticut*, U.S. Supreme Court, June 7, 1965.

be made by the Connecticut state legislature. He argues that the decision is "dangerous" and could eventually threaten the "tranquility and stability of the nation."

I agree with my Brother [Justice Potter] Stewart's dissenting opinion. And, like him, I do not to any extent whatever base my view that this Connecticut law is constitutional on a belief that the law is wise, or that its policy is a good one. In order that there may be no room at all to doubt why I vote as I do, I feel constrained to add that the law is every bit as offensive to me as it is to my Brethren of the majority and my Brothers [John Marshall] Harlan, [Byron] White and [Arthur] Goldberg, who, reciting reasons why it is offensive to them, hold it unconstitutional. There is no single one of the graphic and eloquent strictures and criticisms fired at the policy of this Connecticut law either by the Court's opinion or by those of my concurring Brethren to which I cannot subscribe— except their conclusion that the evil qualities they see in the law make it unconstitutional.

The Court's Decision Belittles the Fourth Amendment

Had the doctor defendant here, or even the nondoctor defendant, been convicted for doing nothing more than expressing opinions to persons coming to the clinic that certain contraceptive devices, medicines or practices would do them good and would be desirable, or for telling people how devices could be used, I can think of no reasons at this time why their expressions of views would not be protected by the First and Fourteenth Amendments, which guarantee freedom of speech.... But speech is one thing; conduct and physical activities are quite another.... The two defendants here were active participants in an organization which gave physical examinations to women, advised them what kind of contraceptive devices or medicines would most likely be satisfactory for them, and then supplied the devices themselves, all for a graduated scale of fees, based on the family income. Thus, these defendants admittedly engaged with others in a planned course of conduct to help people violate the Connecticut law. Merely because some speech was used in carrying on that conduct—just as, in ordinary life, some speech accompanies most kinds of conduct—we are not, in my view, justified in holding that the First Amendment forbids the State to punish their conduct. Strongly as I desire to protect all First Amendment freedoms, I am unable to stretch the Amendment so as to afford protection to the conduct of these defendants in violating the Connecticut law. What would be the constitutional fate of the law if hereafter applied to punish nothing but speech is, as I have said, quite another matter. The Court talks about a constitutional "right of privacy" as though there is some constitutional provision or provisions forbidding any law ever to be passed which might abridge the "privacy" of individuals. But there is not. There are, of course, guarantees in certain specific constitutional provisions which are designed in part to protect privacy at certain times and places with respect to certain activities. Such, for example, is the Fourth Amendment's guarantee against "unreasonable searches and seizures." But I think it belittles that Amendment to talk about it as though it protects nothing but "privacy." To treat it that way is to give it a niggardly interpretation, not the kind of liberal reading I think any Bill of Rights provision should be given. The average man would very likely not have his feelings soothed any more by having his property seized openly than by having it seized privately and by stealth. He simply wants his property left alone. And a person can be just as much, if not more, irritated, annoyed and injured by an unceremonious public arrest by a policeman as he is by a seizure in the privacy of his office or home.

"Privacy" Is Broad, Abstract, and Ambiguous

One of the most effective ways of diluting or expanding a constitutionally guaranteed right is to substitute for the crucial word or words of a constitutional guarantee another word or words, more or less flexible and more or less restricted in meaning. This fact is well illustrated by the use of the term "right of privacy" as a comprehensive substitute for the Fourth Amendment's guarantee against "unreasonable searches and seizures." "Privacy" is a broad, abstract and ambiguous concept which can easily be shrunken in meaning but which can also, on the other hand, easily be interpreted as a constitutional ban against many things other than searches and seizures. I have expressed the view many times that First Amendment freedoms, for example, have suffered from a failure of the courts to stick to the simple language of the First Amendment in construing it, instead of invoking multitudes of words substituted for those the Framers used. For these reasons, I get nowhere in this case by talk about a constitutional "right of privacy" as an emanation from one or more constitutional provisions. I like my privacy as well as the next one, but I am nevertheless compelled to admit that government has a right to invade it unless prohibited by some specific constitutional provision. For these reasons, I cannot agree with the Court's judgment and the reasons it gives for holding this Connecticut law unconstitutional.

> "[Legal scholar Robert] Bork's critique
> of Griswold certainly did not prevail,
> but it did smooth the way for other le-
> gal commentators who similarly advo-
> cated scholarly and judicial rejection of
> the decision."

Precursors to and Criticisms of *Griswold*

David J. Garrow

David J. Garrow is a historian and senior research fellow at Homerton College, University of Cambridge. In the following ex-cerpt from this full-length study of the fifty-year struggle behind the Supreme Court's 1973 Roe v. Wade *decision guaranteeing a woman's right to abortion, Garrow discusses the criticisms of the* Griswold v. Connecticut *decision.* Griswold *deemed that a right to privacy could be found in the Constitution that invalidated an 1879 Connecticut law prohibiting the distribution of contra-ceptive materials. Garrow discusses the precursors to the case be-fore detailing the positions of those who embraced and shunned the ruling. Garrow focuses on the views of the conservative American legal scholar Robert Bork, who shaped much later thinking about the case.*

On February 11 Tom Emerson filed a ninety-six-page brief on behalf of Estelle Griswold and Lee Buxton with the Supreme Court. It was an impressive if not exhaustive piece of work, especially in light of the suddenness with which it had

David J. Garrow, "Creating the Right to Privacy: Estelle Griswold and the U.S. Supreme Court, 1961–65," Liberty and Sexuality: The Right to Privacy and the Making of Roe v. Wade, Updated, Macmillan Publishing Company, 1998. Copyright © 1994 by David J. Garrow. All rights reserved. Reproduced by permission of the author.

had to be prepared, and it offered two main arguments: first, that the 1879 law contravened the liberty protected by the Fourteenth Amendment, and, second, that its application to Griswold and Buxton also violated their First Amendment freedom of speech. Emerson subsumed the privacy argument into the liberty one. "The Connecticut statutes violate due process in that they constitute an unwarranted invasion of privacy. Whether one derives the right of privacy from a composite of the Third, Fourth and Fifth Amendments, from the Ninth Amendment, or from the 'liberty' clause of the Fourteenth Amendment, such a constitutional right has been specifically recognized by this Court. Although the boundaries of this constitutional right of privacy have not yet been spelled out, plainly the right extends to unwarranted government invasion of (1) the sanctity of the home, and (2) the intimacies of the sexual relationship in marriage. These core elements of the right to privacy are combined in this case."

The Arguments of the Briefs

Emerson critically surveyed the possible legislative purposes which may have underlain the 1879 enactments, noted how widespread the acceptance of birth control now was within American society, and then returned to his argument that the First, Third, Fourth, and Fifth Amendments taken in tandem "embody a general principle which protects the private sector of life." Additionally, "the interest of married spouses in the sanctity and privacy of their marital relations involves precisely the kind of right which the Ninth Amendment was intended to secure." All told, Emerson concluded, "the demands of modern life require that the composite of these specific protections be accorded the status of a recognized constitutional right," and reiterated again that "the sanctity of the home and the wholly personal nature of marital relations" together form "the inner core of the right of privacy."

The four supportive amicus briefs were filed soon after Emerson's, and were generally unremarkable. [Harriet] Pilpel and [Nancy] Wechsler, on behalf of PPFA [Planned Parenthood Federation of America], emphasized the extensive popular approval now accorded birth control, and [Whitney] Seymour's brief for the doctors repeated well-known themes. Robert Fleming for the Catholic Council on Civil Liberties emphasized that the right of privacy was "within the liberty protected by the Fourteenth Amendment," and the ACLU's [American Civil Liberties Union's] submission highlighted exactly the same point. Earlier Court decisions such as *Meyer [v. Nebraska]* and *Pierce [v. Society of Sisters]* recognized "marriage and the family as the ultimate repository of personal freedom," and reaching beyond those previous holdings stood "the wife's right to order her childbearing according to her financial and emotional needs, her abilities, and her achievements."

The amicus briefs, especially the Catholic one, drew a significant amount of press attention, and the attorneys on each side had a fairly good sense of where they stood. Joe Clark replied to one law student's inquiry by remarking that "I have the good fortune, or lack thereof, to be" arguing *Griswold* for the state, while Tom Emerson expressed considerable optimism in response to the persnickety Morris Ernst. Harriet Pilpel notified Emerson that she was asking the Court for thirty minutes of oral argument time for herself in addition to the one hour each that both Emerson and Clark would have, although she acknowledged that the chances of the Court granting her request were "virtually nil."

On March 11 Joe Clark submitted his brief in defense of the 1879 statute, a thirty-four-page effort that attempted to find a variety of procedural flaws in the case while also asserting that "There has been no invasion of anyone's privacy in this case." Although it was not apposite, Clark also volunteered that any suggestion "that single people should be allowed to use a contraceptive device is so contra to American experience, thought, and family law that it does not merit further discussion." Five days after Clark's filing, the clerk's office informed all parties that the oral argument of *Griswold v. Connecticut* would commence on March 29 and that Pilpel's request to participate had been denied. . . .

The Justices' Considerations

The private conference discussion of *Griswold* by the nine justices took place . . . on Friday, April 2. Some of the justices, such as John Harlan and William Douglas, knew without a moment's doubt how they felt about the case. But Earl Warren was highly uncertain, and in advance of the conference he looked over the long memo that John Ely had given him four weeks earlier, and sketched out his own reactions. First, "I would give the Legis[lature] a chance to dispose of it by waiting, if possible, to adjournment," to see whether the 1965 Connecticut General Assembly might amend or repeal it. Second, [Chief Justice Earl] Warren was certain of several things he could not do. "I cannot say that it affects the 1st Amend[ment] rights of doctors." Additionally, "I cannot say the state has no legitimate interest—that would lead me to trouble on abortions." Also, "I cannot balance the interest of the state against that of the individual," and "I cannot use the substantive due process approach." Likewise, "I do not believe the equal protection argument is sound," and "I do not accept the privacy argument." The Chief Justice realized that did not leave him with many other options, and Ely's recommendation might be the best course: Warren could support voiding the law either "on a *Yick Wo* theory or on the basis that the statute is not tightly drawn."

Earl Warren

When the April 2 discussion of *Griswold* commenced, the Chief [Justice Earl Warren] articulated to his colleagues most of the thoughts he had jotted down to himself. He was "bothered with the case," and certainly held out some hope that the Connecticut legislature "may repeal the law." He "can't say it affects the First Amendment rights of doctors," and "can't say the state has no interest in the field," for such a holding "could apply to abortion laws." Warren further recited that he could not employ substantive due process or equal protection, and could not accept a privacy argument. Then he explained that he might rely upon *Yick Wo* [*v. Hopkins* (1886)] since there was no effective prohibition on contraceptive sales in Connecticut and since prosecutors did not "go after doctors as such but only clinics." He would favor an opinion saying that any statute regulating the practice of contraception had to be clearly, carefully, and narrowly drawn, since basic rights were involved—"we are dealing with a confidential association, the most intimate in our life."

Hugo Black

Hugo Black spoke next, and from the tenor of his questions to Emerson, none of his colleagues doubted where Black would come out, his apparent dissent in *Poe* [*v. Ullman* (1961)] notwithstanding. He could not vote to reverse on any ground, Black said, not on a First Amendment speech basis or on any freedom of association claim. The First Amendment right of association, Black explained, "is for me the right of assembly, and the right of husband and wife to assemble in bed is a new right of assembly to me." He could not see why the statute was not within the state's power to enact, and while he was open to being shown that the law might somehow be unconstitutionally vague, he was firmly opposed to any due process balancing analysis of the case.

William Douglas

William O. Douglas immediately challenged Black's comments. The right of association is more than a right of assembly, Douglas explained; it is a right to join with and associate with others. A right to send a child to a nonpublic school, as in *Pierce*, was on the periphery of the First Amendment right to association, just as the Court had held that the right to travel also lay within the periphery of First Amendment protection. So too was this present right of association, for there was nothing more personal than this relationship, and even on the periphery it was within First Amendment protection.

Tom Clark

Four years earlier Tom Clark, like Earl Warren, had joined the Frankfurter opinion in *Poe*, but now he firmly and succinctly agreed with Douglas. Alluding to *Meyer* and to *Pierce*, he said that there was a right to marry, to maintain a home, and to have children. This indeed was an area where people have the "right to be let alone." Hugo Black interrupted him to assert that "a state can abolish marriage," but Clark let the remark pass and reiterated his position—this was an area where people have the right to be let alone, and he preferred that principle as the grounds for reversing the Connecticut convictions.

John Harlan

The ageing John Harlan restated his position from *Poe v. Ullman*. He would reverse on the basis of Fourteenth Amendment due process liberty, but he noted that he would feel differently if the Connecticut law were not a 'use' statute and did not apply to married couples.

Next, Bill Brennan, who had been the decisive swing vote in *Poe*, briefly said that he agreed with the Chief, Clark, and Douglas, and favored reversal because of how the statute infringed upon the realm of privacy.

Potter Stewart

But Potter Stewart, who had clearly intimated in *Poe* that he shared Bill Douglas's and John Harlan's objections to the Connecticut statute, now said that he could not find anything in the Bill of Rights that touched upon this. Nothing in Amendments One, Three, Four, Five, Nine or in any others prohibited such a statute, and hence he would have to vote to affirm. The place to get relief from the 1879 statute, Stewart said, was in the Connecticut legislature.

Byron White

The eighth justice to speak was Byron R. White. Nominated to the Court in 1962 to take the seat of the retiring Charles E. Whittaker, White was best known as a former college football star from the late 1930s rather than for his role in Kennedy's presidential campaign and his one year as Deputy Attorney General. After service in World War II and graduation from Yale Law School, White had clerked for Chief Justice Fred M. Vinson and had then practiced law in Denver until being drawn into Kennedy's Justice Department. He had been on the Court for less than three years at the time *Griswold* was argued, compiling an unremarkable and sometimes unpredictable voting record. On *Griswold* he told his colleagues simply that he too would vote to reverse.

Arthur Goldberg

The ninth and most junior justice was Arthur J. Goldberg, Kennedy's Secretary of Labor until he was named to succeed the retiring Felix Frankfurter five months after White had replaced Whittaker. A 1929 graduate of Northwestern University Law School, Goldberg had had a highly distinguished career as a labor lawyer before taking the post in Kennedy's cabinet. While White in his two years plus had become best known within the Court for his rough approach to basketball, Goldberg had quickly emerged as an intellectually active and effervescent justice who had developed especially good relationships with Brennan, Warren, and Harlan.

On *Griswold*, Goldberg said that he too favored reversal, relying on *Meyer* and *Pierce*. Connecticut had no compelling interest that justified the 1879 statute, and the law clearly infringed upon associational rights as protected by the First Amendment. Two fairly recent cases involving penalties imposed upon former or present Communist Party members, *Schware v. Board of Bar Examiners* and *Aptheker v. Secretary of State*, had involved parallel concerns, Goldberg said, and if one had the right to join a political organization then one "can join his wife and live with her as he likes."

At the end of that discussion, the tally on *Griswold* was clear and straightforward: seven votes for reversing the convictions and two principled votes—Black and Stewart—against any reversal. The following Monday morning Earl Warren circulated the assignment list for new opinions, and to the dismay of at least one or two chambers, *Griswold v. Connecticut* was assigned to William O. Douglas. . . .

Precursors to the Privacy Finding

The constitutional right to privacy created by the Supreme Court in *Griswold*, as Tom Emerson's doctrinal comments clearly reflected, was not without suggestive precursors. Thomas Cooley's 1888 coining of the "right to be let alone" was among the best known, but even "the right to privacy" itself, although in a very different legal application than that of *Griswold*, had already been quietly present on the American legal scene for three quarters of a century. Less than two years after Cooley's treatise appeared, a well-known journalist writing in *Scribner's Magazine*, E. L. Godkin, first spoke of "the right to privacy" in the context of criticizing personally salacious and intrusive newspaper reporting. Five months later two young Boston lawyers, Samuel D. Warren and Louis D. Brandeis, used that simple phrase as the title for a *Harvard Law Review* essay that discussed how "political, social, and economic changes entail the recognition of new rights" and called for affirmation of "a general right to privacy for thoughts, emotions, and sensations." Like Godkin, it was "the unwarranted invasion of individual privacy" by the press that troubled Warren and Brandeis, and in calling for shielding of "the private life, habits, acts, and relations of an individual" they emphasized that "the general object is to protect the privacy of private life." Their advocacy of new statutory protection against the excesses of the "yellow" press drew widespread approbation, but neither popular magazines such as *The Nation* nor professional journals such as the *Northwestern Law Review* saw much chance for actual legislative action that would open way for tort law civil damage suits against irresponsible publications.

Warren and Brandeis's article generated considerable ongoing attention in legal circles, and several years later Augustus N. Hand—who in 1936 would author the landmark federal circuit court opinion in *United States v. One Package*—enthusiastically endorsed their argument, saying that privacy was "an extension if not a part" of what he termed "the right of personal liberty." In 1902, however, New York's top court in a 4 to 3 ruling in *Abigail Roberson v. Rochester Folding Box Co.* refused to apply the Warren and Brandeis concept on behalf of a young woman whose permission had not been sought or attained before her photograph was employed as an illustration in a baking products advertisement which characterized either her and/or the product as the "flour of the family." That decision met with "a storm of professional, as well as popular, disapproval," and three years later the Supreme Court of Georgia, in the first ever victory for a tort law right of privacy, ruled in favor of an Atlanta man, Paolo Pavesich, who had filed suit after a life insurance company had used his picture in an advertisement without permission. "Each person has a liberty of privacy," the Georgia court declared, "derived from natural law" and protected by the constitutional language of due process. "The right of privacy has its foundation in the instincts of nature. It is recognized intuitively, consciousness being the witness that can be called to establish its existence."

Pavesich v. New England Life Insurance Co. was welcomed and praised throughout the legal profession, and by the time Louis D. Brandeis joined the U.S. Supreme Court in 1916 the privacy concept he had helped introduce a quarter century earlier was slowly gaining official favor. Even before his arrival the high court had given some form of passing recognition to personal privacy on at least three occasions, and even in advance of his well-known statement in the 1928 wiretapping case of *Olmstead v. United States*, Brandeis had occasion to speak of "the privacy and freedom of the home" in a 1920 dissent. His *Olmstead* statement was only of persuasive, not precedental value, for no other justice joined him in it, and it was made wholly within the bounds of the Fourth Amendment's prohibition against "unreasonable searches and seizures," but it nonetheless became a much-celebrated declaration of individual civil liberties. The framers of the Constitution, Brandeis said, "conferred, as against the Government, the right to be let alone—the most comprehensive of rights and the right most valued by civilized men. To protect that right, every unjustifiable intrusion by the Government upon the privacy of the individual, whatever the means employed, must be deemed a violation of the Fourth Amendment."

Criticisms of the Decision

One perceptive commentator, Robert G. Dixon, took issue with some of the simple rhetorical labels that might be applied to *Griswold*, pointing out that "The privacy issue" is not "simply a right to be let alone; rather, it takes on an aspect of an affirmative right of access to information concerning a very private sphere of life," for "information relevant to marital privacies is what *Griswold* . . . comes down to." Dixon explained that "By invoking the married couples' fictional fear of prosecution for *use* of contraceptives to give the clinic defendants standing to defend themselves from actual prosecution for giving *advice*, the Court tied marital privacy and access to information together into a single bundle of rights." He emphasized that "unless some kind of information-access theory is recognized as implicit in *Griswold*, then it stands as a decision without a satisfying rationale."

But a significant proportion of law school critics were troubled by Douglas's "curious, puzzling mixture of reasoning" and by its "ambiguous and uncertain" reach. One splenetic commentator attacked *Griswold* as "a malformation of constitutional law which thrives because of the conceptual vacuum surrounding the legal notion of privacy," but more common complaints were that the opinion was "far from satisfying," "shot through with serious weaknesses," or "rather opaque." "Only the rhapsody on marriage," one subsequent writer opined, "saves an opinion whose concepts fall suddenly in a heap."

Some *Griswold* critics focused upon Douglas's and especially Arthur Goldberg's utilization of the Ninth Amendment, while others drew a particular bead on Douglas's use of the term "penumbra." Originally coined by astronomer Johannes Kepler in 1604 to describe the area of partial or shaded illumination occasioned by an eclipse, many commentators found Douglas's use of the spatial metaphor "obfuscating rather than clarifying," even though—as many critics failed to realize—the term already had been employed more than twenty times in previous Supreme Court opinions. Oliver Wendell Holmes had used it in an 1873 law review article—"the penumbra between darkness and light"—then employed it three times at the turn of the century while on the Massachusetts Supreme Judicial Court, and subsequently utilized it in four Supreme Court opinions, including a dissent of his own in *Olmstead v. United States*, where he spoke of "the penumbra of the Fourth and Fifth Amendments." Learned Hand, Benjamin Cardozo, and Douglas himself had all employed "penumbra" on multiple earlier occasions, and even Felix Frankfurter had used it once. One of the most perceptive students of *Griswold* later

noted that "Douglas could have replaced penumbra with periphery or fringe with no loss of meaning or force," but his
usage of so unusual a word in such a central role in the opinion became an easy target for those whose objections to either
Douglas's formulation or the decision itself were otherwise
more diffuse.

Robert Bork

Within a half-dozen years of the decision, however, a one-time
Yale Law School colleague of both Fowler Harper and Tom
Emerson emerged as *Griswold's* most prominent and outspo-
ken critic. Originally Robert H. Bork had started out as a
rather pronounced fan of the ruling. Writing in 1968 he had
conceded that Douglas's opinion was "shallow, murky," "rhetorical" and of "poor quality," but nonetheless Douglas and
the Court's basic "idea of deriving new rights from old is valid
and valuable. The construction of new rights can start from
existing constitutional guarantees, particularly the first eight
amendments, which may properly be taken as specific examples of the general set of natural rights contemplated" by
the Framers and specifically by the Ninth Amendment. Out of
that base, Bork explained, "the judge can construct principles
that explain existing constitutional rights and extrapolate
from them to define new natural rights," just as the Court in
part had done in *Griswold*.

But within three years Professor Bork's tune had changed
completely. Writing in a 1971 article that became famous
within the legal profession long before its author became a
public figure, Bork expressly retracted his 1968 remarks and
now insisted that a judge "must stick close to the text and the
history, and their fair implications, and not construct new
rights." *Griswold's* right to privacy, he now explained, "fails every test of neutrality. The derivation of the principle was utterly specious, and so was its definition. In fact, we are left
with no idea of what the principle really forbids." That meant

that *Griswold* "is an unprincipled decision, both in the way in which it derives a new constitutional right and in the way it defines that right, or rather fails to define it," since it provided "no idea of the sweep of the right of privacy and hence no notion of the cases to which it may or may not be applied in the future." *Any* application of due process liberty "is and always has been an improper doctrine," and "Courts must accept any value choice the legislature makes unless it clearly runs contrary to a choice made in the framing of the Constitution."

In subsequent years Bork further intensified his attack on *Griswold*, telling one audience in 1982 that "The result in *Griswold* could not have been reached by proper interpretation of the Constitution" and a 1985 interviewer that "I don't think there is a supportable method of constitutional reasoning underlying the *Griswold* decision." Two years later Bork had occasion to expand on his feelings, explaining that *Griswold* was "not a case of Connecticut going out and doing anything" to enforce the 1879 statute, but had been cooked up by his Yale Law School colleagues "because they like this kind of litigation." "The only reason" the "utterly antique" Connecticut law had "stayed on the statute book was that it was not enforced," Bork explained. "If anybody had tried to enforce that against a married couple, he would have been out of office instantly and the law would have been repealed." However, "some professors found that law in the books and tried to frame a case to challenge it on constitutional grounds," but "they had trouble getting anybody arrested." Then, after *Poe*, they had "engaged in enormous efforts to get somebody prosecuted," and "they had a terrible time, the Yale professors did, getting these doctors arrested." The "only person who could get arrested was a doctor who advertised that he was giving birth control information," Bork went on, "and the thing was really a test case on an abstract principle." "I think both sides regarded it as an interesting test case. The whole case was practically an academic exercise."

Criticisms Intensify

Bork willingly conceded that "the Connecticut law was an outrage and it would have been more of an outrage if they ever enforced it against an individual." If faced with such a law as a legislator, "I would vote against that statute instantly," for with regard to *Griswold's* result, "I agreed with it politically." Bork also concurred that "No civilized person wants to live in a society without a lot of privacy in it," and acknowledged that the framers of the Constitution "protected privacy in a variety of ways" in a number of provisions in the Bill of Rights. "There is a lot of privacy in the Constitution," and "as to the marital right of privacy, I think it is essential to a civilized society." Indeed, "I think marital privacy is a right older than the Bill of Rights."

But "the mere fact that a law is outrageous is not enough to make it unconstitutional," Bork explained. Moreover, Justice Douglas's specter of police searches of marital bedrooms in *Griswold* was "wholly bizarre and imaginary," for "privacy was not the issue in that case. It was the use of contraceptives." There was a much more basic problem with *Griswold*, however, for "the right of privacy, as defined or undefined by Justice Douglas, was a free-floating right that was not derived in a principled fashion from constitutional materials." Douglas's right to privacy "does not having any rooting in the Constitution" and instead "comes out of nowhere." Bork sought to explain that "it is not a right of privacy I am opposed to. It is a generalized, undefined right of privacy that is not drawn from any constitutional provision." "I certainly would not accept emanations and penumbras analysis, which is I think less an analysis than a metaphor," and in *Griswold* he would have joined Justices Black and Stewart in dissent. . . .

A "Spurious Right"

Two years later, and with much more time available to insure the accuracy of his comments, Bork asserted that "the spurious right of privacy that *Griswold* created" had arisen from a case involving "two doctors" where "the lawyers had a difficult time getting the state even to fine two doctors as accessories." "Anyone who reads *Griswold* can see that it was not an adjustment of an old principle to a new reality but the creation of a new principle by *tour de force* or, less politely, by sleight of hand." Contending that "the reasoning of *Griswold* was not meant to be taken seriously by judges, only by the general public," Bork also went out of his way to expressly reject John Harlan's landmark dissent in *Poe* as well as the opinions in *Griswold*: "Harlan's arguments were entirely legislative. The stark fact is that the Constitution has nothing whatever to do with issues of sexual morality," and "*Poe v. Ullman* led directly to the intellectual catastrophe of *Griswold*."

Bork's critique of *Griswold* certainly did not prevail, but it did smooth the way for other legal commentators who similarly advocated scholarly and judicial rejection of the decision. One law journal writer, explaining that "the Court and the American polity have been ill-served by the creation of a general constitutional right of privacy," insisted that "it is time to cast *Griswold* aside" and contended that "no reason exists for not leaving the resolution of privacy-related issues to the political branches." An undistinguished but often-quoted one-time Justice Department official and op-ed contributor called *Griswold* "one of the worst decisions the court ever handed down" and later seemed to suggest that Griswold and Buxton's convictions indeed should have been affirmed rather than voided on "utterly incomprehensible" grounds. A serious legal historian, while conceding that the Connecticut statute was "utterly unreasonable," nevertheless termed *Griswold* the single "most egregious example" of excessive Warren Court activism. And the Solicitor General of the United States in the early 1980s called *Griswold* "pernicious" and explained that "the Court was basically wrong to infer a general right of privacy from shadows allegedly cast by the Bill of Rights . . . We have to accept that there's a difference between laws that embody bad policy and laws that a state legislature lacks the power to enact. A law can be bad—like the Connecticut law in *Griswold*—without being unconstitutional."

"[T]he justices in Griswold produced a
non-text-based and generalized right.
'Privacy' functioned as a euphemism
for immunity from those public-morals
laws deemed by the justices to reflect
benighted moral views."

Griswold Was a Manipulation
of Constitutional Law

Robert P. George and David L. Tubbs

*Robert P. George is McCormick Professor of Jurisprudence and
director of the James Madison Program in American Ideals and
Institutions at Princeton University. David L. Tubbs is a visiting
fellow in social and political studies at the American Enterprise
Institute. In the following viewpoint, the authors discuss the impact of* Griswold v. Connecticut *forty years after it was decided.
The Court ruled in favor of the appellants Estelle Griswold and
C. Lee Buxton, finding that the Connecticut law under which
they were convicted violated a constitutional right to privacy.
Griswold and Buxton had been dispensing contraceptive materials and advice to married couples from their birth control clinic,
which under an 1879 state statute was illegal. George and Tubbs
believe that although the Supreme Court's decision at the time
seemed harmless enough, its impact over time has been serious.
Later decisions using* Griswold *as a precedent saw the rights at
issue changed, so they became not only rights of married couples
but rights of unmarried peoples and then generalized rights that
encompassed the right to have an abortion under* Roe v. Wade

Robert P. George and David L. Tubbs, "The Bad Decision That Started It All: *Griswold*
at 40," *National Review*, vol. 57, no. 13, July 18, 2005, p. 39. Copyright © 2005 by National Review, Inc., 215 Lexington Avenue, New York, NY 10016. Reproduced by permission

in 1973. The authors point out the myths surrounding the Griswold *decision and call for an admission by the Court that the manipulation of constitutional law that began with* Griswold *has been a colossal mistake.*

Forty years ago, in *Griswold v. Connecticut*, the Supreme Court of the United States struck down state laws forbidding the sale, distribution, and use of contraceptives on the basis of a novel constitutional doctrine known as the "right to marital privacy."

Privacy Right Made Public Policy

At the time, the decision appeared to be harmless. After all, Griswold simply allowed married couples to decide whether to use contraceptives. But the Supreme Court soon transformed the "right to privacy" (the reference to marriage quickly disappeared) into a powerful tool for making public policy. In *Eisenstadt v. Baird* (1972), the Court changed a right of spouses—justified in Griswold precisely by reference to the importance of marriage—into a right of unmarried adults to buy and use contraceptives. Then, in a move that plunged the United States into a "culture war," the Court ruled in *Roe v. Wade* and *Doe v. Bolton* (1973) that this generalized "right to privacy" also encompassed a woman's virtually unrestricted right to have an abortion.

No one doubts that there are true privacy rights in the Constitution, especially in the Fourth Amendment, which protects against unreasonable searches and seizures and ensures that warrants issue only upon a showing of probable cause that a crime has been committed. (Indeed, these rights prevented any kind of aggressive enforcement of the laws struck down in *Griswold.*) But the justices in *Griswold* produced a non-text-based and generalized right. "Privacy" functioned as a euphemism for immunity from those public-morals laws deemed by the justices to reflect benighted moral views.

Silencing of Criticism

The privacy decisions that sprang from *Griswold* have been widely criticized, and in the last 20 years there have been two notable efforts to silence and stigmatize that criticism. The first occurred in 1987, when a coalition of liberal interest groups helped to scotch Judge Robert Bork's nomination to the Supreme Court, partly because of Bork's misgivings about this novel doctrine. The second occurred in 1992, when the Supreme Court decided *Planned Parenthood v. Casey*, which reaffirmed the "central holding" of *Roe v. Wade*.

Neither of these efforts succeeded. To this day, millions of Americans cannot accept *Roe v. Wade* as constitutionally legitimate. And thanks to recent developments, public suspicion of the Court's "privacy" doctrine is now greater than ever.

Two years ago, in *Lawrence v. Texas*, the Supreme Court pushed the doctrine into new territory by overruling *Bowers v. Hardwick* (1986), a decision that had upheld a state's authority to prohibit homosexual sodomy. But in *Lawrence*, Justice Anthony Kennedy provocatively remarked that *Bowers* was wrong the day it was decided. Criticism of the ruling in *Lawrence* intensified a few months later when the supreme judicial court of Massachusetts promulgated a right to same-sex marriage in that state. In *Goodridge v. Department of Public Health* (2003), the court cited *Lawrence* to support this newly minted right. It evidently mattered little to these judges that the majority opinion in *Lawrence* expressly denied that the case involved the issue of marriage.

Griswold Must Be Reexamined

As the courts push the "privacy" doctrine further and further, public criticism keeps pace. *Griswold*, however, has received little attention. Even harsh critics of *Roe* and *Lawrence* are loath to say that *Griswold* was wrongly decided. Most of those who worry about the judicial abuse of the right to privacy do not want or expect the Supreme Court to revisit the case. Yet the cogency of any serious critique of "privacy" may depend on the willingness to reexamine the roots of the doctrine in *Griswold*.

Consider abortion. Conceding the correctness of *Griswold* gives a huge advantage to the defenders of *Roe* and *Casey*. They benefit because so many influential jurists and scholars say that the "inner logic" of the contraception cases must yield something like *Roe*. Outsiders may regard this argument with skepticism, but its purpose is clear: It tries to smooth the road from *Griswold* to *Eisenstadt* to *Roe*—and beyond.

But one point is rarely mentioned. Even though *Griswold* was less consequential than *Roe*, the two cases suffer from similar flaws. The many shortcomings of *Griswold* are less well known, because the case is enveloped in myths.

The Law and "Lifestyle Liberalism"

In American law schools, decisions such as *Roe, Casey*, and *Lawrence* are widely praised—not because of their legal merits (which are dubious), but because they comport with the ideology of "lifestyle liberalism" that enjoys hegemony there. Consequently, since 1973 most legal scholars have had no incentive to reassess *Griswold*. But if *Griswold* was wrongly decided, *Roe*—intellectually shaky on any account—loses even the meager jurisprudential support on which it rests.

Myths Surrounding *Griswold*

The lack of scholarly engagement with *Griswold* partly explains the myths now surrounding it. Exposing those myths further undermines the arguments for a generalized right to privacy.

Myth # 1: The Connecticut laws were "purposeless restraints," serving no social interest.

Supreme Court Justice David Souter is one of several jurists to make this assertion. The confusion arises from *Griswold*, whose majority opinion nowhere identifies a legislative purpose.

For anyone who cares to look, the purposes of the laws are apparent in the record of the case: Connecticut sought to promote marital fidelity and stable families by discouraging attempts to avoid the possible consequences of non-marital sexual relations through the use of contraceptives. Prominent judges in Connecticut recognized the legitimacy of these purposes, and the state's supreme court upheld the laws against several constitutional challenges from 1940 to 1964.

Did Connecticut's policy go too far in its efforts to promote marital fidelity? Many thought so. But roughly 30 states regulated contraceptives in the early 1960s, and the uniqueness of Connecticut's statutory scheme was long recognized as its constitutional prerogative.

Myth #2: The decision in *Griswold* rested on some overarching or time-honored constitutional principle.

Ostensibly, that principle was privacy. But the *Griswold* doctrine would have been unrecognizable to the Supreme Court even a few years earlier. In *Gardner v. Massachusetts* (1938), for example, the Court dismissed a similar challenge, noting that the suit failed to present "a substantial federal question."

In the majority opinion in *Griswold*, Justice William O. Douglas referred—as comically metaphysical as it sounds—to "penumbras formed by emanations" of specific constitutional guarantees as the source of the new right. He had nothing else to go on.

Other jurists have since argued that the right to marital privacy could be derived from cases before 1965 involving the rights of parents to direct the upbringing of their children. But the cases they cite have little in common with *Griswold*.

What, then, was the operative "principle" in *Griswold*? Nothing other than the Court's desire to place its imprimatur on "enlightened" views about human sexuality. This project continued beyond *Griswold* and culminated in *Lawrence*, where the Court essentially said that all adults in America have a right to engage in consenting, non-marital sexual relations. Consistently missing from the Court's discourse on privacy, however, has been any discussion of parental duties, public health, and the welfare of children.

Myth #3: No sensible jurist or commentator would say that the case was wrongly decided.

In fact, two widely respected and sensible jurists, Justices Hugo Black and Potter Stewart, dissented in *Griswold*. Black was a noted liberal and, like Stewart, recorded his opposition to Connecticut's policy as a political matter. Yet both jurists insisted that the policy was a valid exercise of the state's power to promote public health, safety, and morals.

To Justices Black and Stewart, the "right to privacy" cloaked a naked policy preference. Justices in the majority were, without constitutional warrant, substituting their own judgments for those of the elected representatives in Connecticut. This, according to jurists across the political spectrum, is precisely what had brought shame on the Court during the "*Lochner* [*v. New York* (1905)] era," from roughly 1890 to 1937, when in the name of an unwritten "liberty of contract" the justices invalidated state social-welfare and worker-protection laws. But the crucial distinction underscored by Black and Stewart between the desirability or justice of a policy and the state's constitutional authority to enact it lost much of its currency as the right to privacy expanded.

Myth #4: The legislation invalidated in *Griswold* might be widely used again if the case was overturned.

This line was often repeated in 1987 when Robert Bork was nominated to the Supreme Court. Meant to frighten ordinary citizens who approve of contraceptive use, this scenario simply fails to acknowledge changes in public opinion since 1965. Laws like those struck down in *Griswold* clearly have little chance of passing today even in the most conservative states.

Myth #5: The widespread use of contraceptives in the United States today provides a post hoc justification for *Griswold*.

When *Griswold* was decided, adults could buy and use contraceptives in almost every state (despite various regulations on their sale and distribution). Given the social ferment of the 1960s and '70s, the Connecticut policy would sooner or later have been modified. But the ubiquity of contraceptives in America today does not justify *Griswold*—any more than the widespread use of abortion justifies *Roe*.

Repudiating the Generalized Right to Privacy

It might seem fanciful to say that the idea of a generalized constitutional right to "privacy" could now be repudiated; many believe that it has become an integral part of American law. But no one should accept this conclusion. The struggle against usurpations by the Supreme Court committed under the pretext of giving effect to unwritten constitutional rights has a historical precedent. As noted, from roughly 1890 to 1937, the Supreme Court invalidated worker-protection and social-welfare legislation on the basis of an unenumerated right to "liberty of contract." After much criticism, the Court relented and in 1937 announced that it would defer to legislative judgment where policies did not run afoul of constitutional principles. They promised, in short, to halt the practice of reading into the Constitution their own personal judgments about social and economic policy and the morality of economic relations.

The Supreme Court will not revisit the question of state or federal laws banning contraceptives. Yet the Court can and should find an occasion to admit that the manipulation of constitutional law that began with *Griswold* has been a colossal mistake. Such an admission would hardly be radical or, as we have observed, unprecedented. The Court's confession of error in repudiating its *Griswold* jurisprudence, far from harming its reputation, would enhance its prestige. We have no doubt that the same good effect would redound to the Court if the justices were candidly to speak the truth: The idea of a generalized right to privacy floating in penumbras formed by emanations was a pure judicial invention—one designed to license the judicial usurpation of democratic legislative authority.

| "Passing years have brought intensified assaults on the right of personal decision making protected by Griswold."

The Right to Privacy Hangs by a Thread

Sarah Weddington and Seth Kretzer

Sarah Weddington, a nationally known attorney and former assistant to the president in the Jimmy Carter White House, argued and won one of the most famous cases in U.S. legal history: Roe v. Wade. Seth Kretzer is an attorney practicing in Houston. In the following viewpoint, they consider the history and future of the right of reproductive privacy. The authors discuss the Griswold v. Connecticut case and Roe v. Wade, expressing concerns that the reproductive rights recognized in those decisions have come under repeated attack. In Griswold, the Court sided with Estelle Griswold and C. Lee Buxton, who ran a birth control clinic, holding that they were wrongfully convicted under a Connecticut law that forbade them to dispense contraceptive devices and advice, because that law violated the right to privacy. Roe v. Wade upheld the right of a woman to continue or terminate a pregnancy. Weddington and Kretzer argue that the rights of women following from these two decisions are in jeopardy for three main reasons: the appointment of two conservative justices to the Supreme Court, Samuel Alito Jr. and John G. Roberts; the increased efforts of states to limit the legality of abortions; and two pending cases involving congressionally established limitations on the availability of abortion.

Sarah Weddington and Seth Kretzer, "Reproductive Privacy Rights: What Direction Does the Chill Wind Blow?" *Human Rights*, vol. 34, no. 1, Winter 2007, pp. 15–17. Copyright © 2007, American Bar Association. Reproduced by permission.

The U.S. Supreme Court decisions of *Griswold v. Connecticut* (1965), and *Roe v. Wade* (1973), recognized the right of a person to decide whether to use contraception and whether to continue or terminate a pregnancy. Passing years have brought intensified assaults on the right of personal decision making protected by *Griswold* and *Roe*. In 1989, in another key reproductive rights case, Justice Harry Blackmun, author of the *Roe* opinion, warned: "For today, the women of this Nation still retain the liberty to control their destinies. But the signs are evident and very ominous, and a chill wind blows" [*Webster v. Reproductive Health Services* (1989)].

Today, ever chillier winds are blowing. The three most salient current concerns are (1) the recent changes in the composition of the Court, with two new justices and the possibility of others; (2) increasing state efforts to limit the legality and availability of abortions; and (3) two cases pending in the Court this term involving congressionally established limitations on the availability of abortions.

New Justices Roberts and Alito

After many years of consistency, the Court changed significantly in 2005. On September 29, following the death of Chief Justice William Rehnquist, who dissented in *Roe* and consistently voted against its principles and progeny, John G. Roberts Jr. became chief justice. Earlier, on July 1, Justice Sandra Day O'Connor had notified President George W. Bush of her decision to retire. During twenty-four terms on the Court, she had become the fulcrum on a 5-4 Court split on reproductive rights cases, generally on the side of respecting the privacy legacy. She remained on the Court until Samuel A. Alito Jr. became the newest associate justice in January 2006.

Although questions at Roberts's and Alito's Senate confirmation hearings frequently had focused on reproductive issues, the hearings did not truly clarify the nominees' positions on those issues. However, there are indications that the new justices will look skeptically on continuing the principles of *Roe*.

We may know more soon. On February 21, 2006, shortly after Alito joined the bench, the Court granted certiorari [agreed to review] to an Eighth Circuit case in *Gonzales v. Carhart*. On June 19, 2006, the Court agreed to hear a second abortion-related case, this one from the Ninth Circuit, *Gonzales v. Planned Parenthood Federation of America, Inc.* The Court heard oral arguments in both cases on November 8, 2006, and most likely will issue its decisions by summer 2007.

Attempts to Limit Abortions

Both *Carhart* and *Planned Parenthood* have their legal roots in the Court's decision in *Stenberg v. Carhart* (2000). That case involved a challenge to the very restrictive abortion law of Nebraska, home to Dr. LeRoy Carhart, one of a handful of doctors nationwide with the expertise to perform an abortion after the first trimester of pregnancy. The 1999 Nebraska law barred most second and third trimester abortions, and in the eight years preceding the *Stenberg* decision, at least thirty other states had passed similar laws. At the federal level, Congress enacted similar prohibitions in both 1996 and 1997, but President Bill Clinton vetoed them, preventing them from becoming law. Proponents of such legislation called the laws "partial birth abortion" statutes; some opponents pejoratively called them "partial abortion ban" statutes.

Ruling on *Stenberg* on June 28, 2000, the Supreme Court found Nebraska's law unconstitutional because it did not contain an exception to allow abortion to protect the health of a pregnant woman. The Court also held that the statutory language was so broad that it covered the vast majority of late term abortions and thus imposed an undue burden on the right to abortion itself.

The Partial-Birth Abortion Ban Act

However, the 2000 elections brought both a new president to the White House and more abortion opponents to Congress. The Partial-Birth Abortion Ban Act of 2003, passed both chambers of Congress by two-to-one margins, and Bush signed it into law. In part, the act exposes "any physician who, in or affecting interstate or foreign commerce, knowingly performs a partial-birth abortion and thereby kills a human fetus" to up to two years of imprisonment.

The act was immediately challenged in three federal courts. All courts that have considered it to date have found it unconstitutional, but not always for the same reasons. The two cases argued on November 8, [2006] generally known as the *Gonzales* cases, therefore could be deciding the scope of reproductive privacy rights for the foreseeable future.

The Constitutionality of the Act

In 2004, the U.S. District Court for the Northern District of California struck down this act and permanently enjoined its enforcement on three separate grounds [*Planned Parenthood Federation of America v. Ashcroft* (2004)]. First, the act was unconstitutionally vague because it could be read to ban other safe, previability second trimester procedures. Second, it did not distinguish between previability and postviability, and therefore imposed an undue burden on a woman's right to choose an abortion. Third, the act's "life exception" did not meet *Stenberg*'s "health exception" requirement. On January 31, 2006, the Ninth Circuit affirmed the lower court holding on all three grounds [*Planned Parenthood Federation of America, Inc. v. Gonzales* (2006)].

Also in 2004, the U.S. District Court for the District of Nebraska held in *Carhart v. Ashcroft* (2004), that "the overwhelming weight of the trial evidence proves that the banned procedure is safe and medically necessary in order to preserve the health of women under certain circumstances. In the absence of an exception for the health of a woman, banning the procedure constitutes a significant health hazard to women." The court added, however, that "[t]he court does not determine whether the Partial-Birth Abortion Ban Act of 2003 is constitutional or unconstitutional when the fetus is indisputably viable." The Eight Circuit affirmed, *Carhart v. Gonzales* (2005), but on narrower grounds than the Ninth Circuit opinion. "Because the Act does not contain a health exception, it is unconstitutional. We therefore do not reach the district court's conclusion of the Act imposing an undue burden on a woman's right to have an abortion."

Future Supreme Court Nominees and the Future of *Roe*

Because the *Gonzales* cases will be the Roberts Court's first major opinions on abortion and privacy, they will receive intense focus and interest. The cases also are likely to spotlight the key role of Justice Anthony Kennedy as the "swing" vote on the Roberts Court, as O'Connor was on the Rehnquist Court.

Speculation also continues about the Court's future makeup. Among those who generally have voted for *Roe*'s progeny are the Court's oldest members, including Justice John Paul Stevens, 87, and Justice Ruth Bader Ginsburg, 74. Any departure from the bench or something else entirely unexpected would create a vacancy, giving Bush the opportunity to appoint another anti-*Roe* justice before he leaves office—or perhaps more than one. However, the fact that Senator Patrick Leahy (D-VT) now heads the Senate Judiciary Committee is likely to have a significant impact on confirmation hearings of future Supreme Court nominees.

Opponents of legalized abortion have been planning ways to take advantage of possible Court changes in their favor. In 2006, the South Dakota legislature passed a bill making all abortion procedures illegal unless necessary to save the life of a pregnant woman. Because similar Texas provisions had been declared unconstitutional in *Roe*, the South Dakota law clearly seemed designed to invite challenges that would give the Court an opportunity to overturn *Roe*. But opponents of this law successfully sought a referendum on the measure in the November 2006 elections, and South Dakota voters rejected the law, 54 percent to 46 percent, despite the state's political profile as a religious, conservative, predominantly Republican state.

The Precarious Future of Privacy Rights

Although that statute was blocked, other contentious issues remain in the public sphere, including access to contraception and emergency contraception and federal funding for clinics created to counsel women against the abortion option. State laws that would lengthen the waiting period for women seeking abortions, change abortion clinic regulations, expand parental notification requirements, or ban abortions in almost all circumstances are being introduced or enacted at a rapid rate.

What would happen if the Court were to overturn *Roe?* Initially, each state's laws would control the legality of abortion in that state, pending possible enactment of any federal legislation on the matter. George Washington University law professor Jeffrey Rosen has predicted that, "in many of the 50 states, and ultimately in Congress, the overturning of *Roe* would probably ignite one of the most explosive political battles since the civil rights movement, if not the Civil War."

The right of privacy . . . seems to hang by a thread. It appears at times that Blackmun's chill wind could become an arctic blast.

CHAPTER 2

Declaring Interracial Marriage Restrictions Unconstitutional

Case Overview

Loving v. Virginia (1967)

Mildred Jeter, a black woman, and Richard Loving, a white man, grew up in Caroline County, Virginia, where they met and fell in love. In 1958, the couple decided to get married, but Virginia law forbade miscegenation, or people of different races to marry each other. Interracial marriage was legal in Washington, D.C., at that time, so the couple traveled to the nation's capital, married, and returned to Virginia to begin their life together.

However, Virginia not only forbade the Lovings from marrying but from living in Virginia as man and wife. One night, as they slept, the police entered the Lovings home and arrested the newly married couple. Their case went to trial, they were found guilty, and were sentenced to a year in jail. However, their sentence would be suspended if they agreed to leave Virginia for twenty-five years. The Lovings, effectively banished from their home, moved to Washington, D.C. But while they could live together legally in Washington, the Lovings faced considerable discrimination as an interracial couple, and without the support of their family in Virginia, they struggled to support their young family. Mildred appealed to the attorney general of the United States, Robert F. Kennedy, for help. His office referred the Lovings to the American Civil Liberties Union (ACLU), who helped them obtain free legal services.

The Lovings' lawyers, Bernard Cohen and Philip Hirschkop, challenged their clients' conviction, arguing that the Virginia miscegenation laws violated their Fourteenth Amendment rights. The Fourteenth Amendment declares that no state shall "deprive any person of life, liberty, or property, without due process of law; nor deny to any person within its jurisdiction the equal protection of the laws." But the original judge in the case, Leon Bazile, upheld his decision, saying, "Almighty God created the races white, black, yellow, Malay and red, and he placed them on separate continents. . . . The fact that he separated the races shows that he did not intend for the races to mix." The case was denied repeatedly in the Virginia courts, which found no discrimination in the case because both parties in the marriage were punished equally. The Lovings' appeal eventually moved all the way up to the United States Supreme Court.

The Supreme Court ruled unanimously in favor of the Lovings, striking down the Virginia statue upon which they had been convicted. In an opinion by Justice Earl Warren, the Court declared that the Virginia law had indeed violated both the due process and equal protection clauses of the Fourteenth Amendment. The Court rejected the Virginia Supreme Court of Appeals' finding that because of "equal application," or equal punishment, there was no racial discrimination, stating that the central purpose of the Fourteenth Amendment is to eliminate all official state sources of invidious racial discrimination and that any law based on racial classification is "suspect." The Court also said that marriage was a basic civil right whose restriction was a violation of the due process clause.

Warren's opinion in *Loving* was consistent with the Court's findings two years earlier in *Griswold v. Connecticut* regarding the protection afforded by the Fourteenth Amendment of fundamental liberties and the rights to privacy. Marriage, according to the Court, is a basic personal liberty that may not be denied. While the Court's decision was directed specifically at the anti-miscegenation laws of Virginia, it was worded broadly enough to strike down the anti-miscegenation laws of fifteen other states as well, which had an immediate and significant cultural and legislative impact. Since then, the ruling has continued to be important to the development of other constitutional policies, especially concerning the protection of marriage and domestic relations. Same-sex marriage advocates invoke *Loving* to argue that a ban on same-sex marriage is a form of sex discrimination, just as a ban on interracial marriage is a form of race discrimination.

> "There can be no doubt that restricting the freedom to marry solely because of racial classifications violates the central meaning of the Equal Protection Clause."

The Court's Decision: Marriage Is a Basic Personal Right

Earl Warren

Earl Warren, a former Republican governor, was appointed to the Supreme Court by President Dwight Eisenhower in 1953. On the bench, Warren was known for his unabashedly liberal stance. The Court decided unanimously in the case of Loving v. Virginia *that a Virginia law preventing marriages between couples solely on the basis of racial classifications violates the Fourteenth Amendment. Mildred Jeter, a black woman, and Richard Loving, a white man, were charged with a felony because they lived together as husband and wife in Caroline County, Virginia. This act was a violation of the state's law against miscegenation, the mixing, cohabitation, or marriage of people of different races. In Warren's opinion, Virginia's miscegenation statutes rest on racial distinctions, and there is no legitimate purpose for these classifications, except for racial discrimination. Thus, these statutes violate the equal protection clause and, in depriving the Lovings of liberty, the due process clause. Warren concludes by asserting that the freedom to marry is one of the vital personal rights that is essential to the pursuit of happiness, and to deny this freedom on the basis of race subverts the principle of equality at the heart of the Fourteenth Amendment.*

Earl Warren, majority opinion, *Loving v. Virginia*, U.S. Supreme Court, June 12, 1967.

This case presents a constitutional question never addressed by this Court: whether a statutory scheme adopted by the State of Virginia to prevent marriages between persons solely on the basis of racial classifications violates the Equal Protection and Due Process Clauses of the Fourteenth Amendment. For reasons which seem to us to reflect the central meaning of those constitutional commands, we conclude that these statutes cannot stand consistently with the Fourteenth Amendment.

Facts of the Case

In June 1958, two residents of Virginia, Mildred Jeter, a Negro woman, and Richard Loving, a white man, were married in the District of Columbia pursuant to its laws. Shortly after their marriage, the Lovings returned to Virginia and established their marital abode in Caroline County. At the October Term, 1958, of the Circuit Court of Caroline County, a grand jury issued an indictment charging the Lovings with violating Virginia's ban on interracial marriages. On January 6, 1959, the Lovings pleaded guilty to the charge and were sentenced to one year in jail; however, the trial judge suspended the sentence for a period of 25 years on the condition that the Lovings leave the State and not return to Virginia together for 25 years. He stated in an opinion that:

> "Almighty God created the races white, black, yellow, Malay and red, and he placed them on separate continents. And but for the interference with his arrangement there would be no cause for such marriages. The fact that he separated the races shows that he did not intend for the races to mix."

After their convictions, the Lovings took up residence in the District of Columbia. On November 6, 1963, they filed a motion in the state trial court to vacate the judgment and set aside the sentence on the ground that the statutes which they had violated were repugnant to the Fourteenth Amendment. The motion not having been decided by October 28, 1964, the

Lovings instituted a class action in the United States District Court for the Eastern District of Virginia requesting that a three-judge court be convened to declare the Virginia antimiscegenation statutes unconstitutional and to enjoin state officials from enforcing their convictions. On January 22, 1965, the state trial judge denied the motion to vacate the sentences, and the Lovings perfected an appeal to the Supreme Court of Appeals of Virginia. On February 11, 1965, the three-judge District Court continued the case to allow the Lovings to present their constitutional claims to the highest state court.

The Supreme Court of Appeals upheld the constitutionally of the antimiscegenation statutes and, after modifying the sentence, affirmed the convictions. The Lovings appealed this decision, and we noted probable jurisdiction on December 12, 1966.

The Virginia Anti-Miscegenation Statutes

The two statutes under which appellants were convicted and sentenced are part of a comprehensive statutory scheme aimed at prohibiting and punishing interracial marriages. The Lovings were convicted of violating 20-58 of the Virginia Code:

> "Leaving State to evade law. If any white person and colored person shall go out of this State, for the purpose of being married, and with the intention of returning, and be married out of it, and afterwards return to and reside in it, cohabiting as man and wife, they shall be punished as provided in 20-59, and the marriage shall be governed by the same law as if it had been solemnized in this State. The fact of their cohabitation here as man and wife shall be evidence of their marriage."

Section 20-59, which defines the penalty for miscegenation, provides:

> "Punishment for marriage. If any white person intermarry with a colored person, or any colored person intermarry

with a white person, he shall be guilty of a felony and shall be punished by confinement in the penitentiary for not less than one nor more than five years."

Other central provisions in the Virginia statutory scheme are 20-57, which automatically voids all marriages between "a white person and a colored person" without any judicial proceeding, and 20-54 and 1-14 which, respectively, define "white persons" and "colored persons and Indians" for purposes of the statutory prohibitions. The Lovings have never disputed in the course of this litigation that Mrs. Loving is a "colored person" or that Mr. Loving is a "white person" within the meanings given those terms by the Virginia statutes.

Virginia is now one of 16 States which prohibit and punish marriages on the basis of racial classifications. Penalties for miscegenation arose as an incident to slavery and have been common in Virginia since the colonial period. The present statutory scheme dates from the adoption of the Racial Integrity Act of 1924, passed during the period of extreme nativism which followed the end of the First World War. The central features of this Act, and current Virginia law, are the absolute prohibition of a "white person" marrying other than another "white person," a prohibition against issuing marriage licenses until the issuing official is satisfied that the applicants' statements as to their race are correct, certificates of "racial composition" to be kept by both local and state registrars, and the carrying forward of earlier prohibitions against racial intermarriage.

Naim v. Naim and Preserving Racial Integrity

In upholding the constitutionality of these provisions in the decision below, the Supreme Court of Appeals of Virginia referred to its 1955 decision in *Naim v. Naim*, as stating the reasons supporting the validity of these laws. In *Naim*, the state court concluded that the State's legitimate purposes were "to preserve the racial integrity of its citizens," and to prevent "the corruption of blood," "a mongrel breed of citizens," and "the obliteration of racial pride," obviously an endorsement of the doctrine of White Supremacy. The court also reasoned that marriage has traditionally been subject to state regulation without federal intervention, and, consequently, the regulation of marriage should be left to exclusive state control by the Tenth Amendment.

Limits on States' Powers to Regulate Marriage

While the state court is no doubt correct in asserting that marriage is a social relation subject to the State's police power, *Maynard v. Hill* (1888), the State does not contend in its argument before this Court that its powers to regulate marriage are unlimited notwithstanding the commands of the Fourteenth Amendment. Nor could it do so in light of *Meyer v. Nebraska* (1923), and *Skinner v. Oklahoma* (1942). Instead, the State argues that the meaning of the Equal Protection Clause, as illuminated by the statements of the Framers, is only that state penal laws containing an interracial element as part of the definition of the offense must apply equally to whites and Negroes in the sense that members of each race are punished to the same degree. Thus, the State contends that, because its miscegenation statutes punish equally both the white and the Negro participants in an interracial marriage, these statutes, despite their reliance on racial classifications, do not constitute an invidious discrimination based upon race. The second argument advanced by the State assumes the validity of its equal application theory. The argument is that, if the Equal Protection Clause does not outlaw miscegenation statutes because of their reliance on racial classifications, the question of constitutionality would thus become whether there was any rational basis for a State to treat interracial marriages differently from other marriages. On this question, the State argues, the scientific evidence is substantially in doubt and, consequently, this

Court should defer to the wisdom of the state legislature in adopting its policy of discouraging interracial marriages.

Justification for Racial Classification Is Required Under the Fourteenth Amendment

Because we reject the notion that the mere "equal application" of a statute containing racial classifications is enough to remove the classifications from the Fourteenth Amendment's proscription of all invidious racial discriminations, we do not accept the State's contention that these statutes should be upheld if there is any possible basis for concluding that they serve a rational purpose. The mere fact of equal application does not mean that our analysis of these statutes should follow the approach we have taken in cases involving no racial discrimination where the Equal Protection Clause has been arrayed against a statute discriminating between the kinds of advertising which may be displayed on trucks in New York City, *Railway Express Agency, Inc. v. New York* (1949), or an exemption in Ohio's ad valorem tax for merchandise owned by a nonresident in a storage warehouse, *Allied Stores of Ohio, Inc. v. Bowers* (1959). In these cases, involving distinctions not drawn according to race, the Court has merely asked whether there is any rational foundation for the discriminations, and has deferred to the wisdom of the state legislatures. In the case at bar, however, we deal with statutes containing racial classifications, and the fact of equal application does not immunize the statute from the very heavy burden of justification which the Fourteenth Amendment has traditionally required of state statutes drawn according to race.

Equal Protection and "Equal Application" Theories

The State argues that statements in the Thirty-ninth Congress about the time of the passage of the Fourteenth Amendment indicate that the Framers did not intend the Amendment to make unconstitutional state miscegenation laws. Many of the statements alluded to by the State concern the debates over the Freedmen's Bureau Bill, which President Johnson vetoed, and the Civil Rights Act of 1866, enacted over his veto. While these statements have some relevance to the intention of Congress in submitting the Fourteenth Amendment, it must be understood that they pertained to the passage of specific statutes and not to the broader, organic purpose of a constitutional amendment. As for the various statements directly concerning the Fourteenth Amendment, we have said in connection with a related problem, that although these historical sources "cast some light" they are not sufficient to resolve the problem; "[a]t best, they are inconclusive. The most avid proponents of the post-War Amendments undoubtedly intended them to remove all legal distinctions among 'all persons born or naturalized in the United States.' Their opponents, just as certainly, were antagonistic to both the letter and the spirit of the Amendments and wished them to have the most limited effect" [*Brown v. Board of Education* (1954). See also *Strauder v. West Virginia* (1880)]. We have rejected the proposition that the debates in the Thirty-ninth Congress or in the state legislatures which ratified the Fourteenth Amendment supported the theory advanced by the State, that the requirement of equal protection of the laws is satisfied by penal laws defining offenses based on racial classifications so long as white and Negro participants in the offense were similarly punished.

The State finds support for its "equal application" theory in the decision of the Court in *Pace v. Alabama* (1883). In that case, the Court upheld a conviction under an Alabama statute forbidding adultery or fornication between a white person and a Negro which imposed a greater penalty than that of a statute proscribing similar conduct by members of the same race. The Court reasoned that the statute could not be said to discriminate against Negroes because the punishment for each participant in the offense was the same. However, as recently as the 1964 Term, in rejecting the reasoning of that case, we stated "Pace represents a limited view of the Equal Protection Clause which has not withstood analysis in the subsequent decisions of this Court" [*McLaughlin v. Florida* (1964)]. As we there demonstrated, the Equal Protection Clause requires the consideration of whether the classifications drawn by any statute constitute an arbitrary and invidious discrimination. The clear and central purpose of the Fourteenth Amendment was to eliminate all official state sources of invidious racial discrimination in the States.

Racial Classification and Equal Protection

There can be no question but that Virginia's miscegenation statutes rest solely upon distinctions drawn according to race. The statutes proscribe generally accepted conduct if engaged in by members of different races. Over the years, this Court has consistently repudiated "[d]istinctions between citizens solely because of their ancestry" as being "odious to a free people whose institutions are founded upon the doctrine of equality" [*Hirabayashi v. United States* (1943)]. At the very least, the Equal Protection Clause demands that racial classifications, especially suspect in criminal statutes, be subjected to the "most rigid scrutiny," [*Korematsu v. United States* (1944)], and, if they are ever to be upheld, they must be shown to be necessary to the accomplishment of some permissible state objective, independent of the racial discrimination which it was the object of the Fourteenth Amendment to eliminate. Indeed, two members of this Court have already stated that they "cannot conceive of a valid legislative purpose . . . which makes the color of a person's skin the test of whether his conduct is a criminal offense" [*McLaughlin v. Florida*, Stewart, J., joined by Douglas, J., concurring].

There is patently no legitimate overriding purpose independent of invidious racial discrimination which justifies this classification. The fact that Virginia prohibits only interracial marriages involving white persons demonstrate, that the racial classifications must stand on their own justification, as measures designed to maintain White Supremacy. We have consistently denied the constitutionality of measures which restrict the rights of citizens on account of race. There can be no doubt that restricting the freedom to marry solely because of racial classifications violates the central meaning of the Equal Protection Clause.

Denying Marriage Rights Based on Racial Classification Subverts Personal Liberty

These statutes also deprive the Lovings of liberty without due process of law in violation of the Due Process Clause of the Fourteenth Amendment. The freedom to marry has long been recognized as one of the vital personal rights essential to the orderly pursuit of happiness by free men.

Marriage is one of the "basic civil rights of man," fundamental to our very existence and survival [*Skinner v. Oklahoma* (1942)]. To deny this fundamental freedom on so unsupportable a basis as the racial classifications embodied in these statutes, classifications so directly subversive of the principle of equality at the heart of the Fourteenth Amendment, is surely to deprive all the State's citizens of liberty without due process of law. The Fourteenth Amendment requires that the freedom of choice to marry not be restricted by invidious racial discriminations. Under our Constitution, the freedom to marry, or not marry, a person of another race resides with the individual and cannot be infringed by the State.

These convictions must be reversed.

"[T]he miscegenation statutes found in seventeen states [in 1966] constitute the last major category of legally enforced discrimination based solely on race."

Arguments for and Against Miscegenation

Walter Wadlington

Walter Wadlington retired as James Madison Professor of Law in 2003, after a forty-year career at the University of Virginia Law School. *In the following excerpt of an essay that was published before the* Loving v. Virginia *decision of 1967, Wadlington offers an analysis of the arguments for and against the constitutionality of miscegenation laws. The* Loving *case involved a couple, Mildred Jeter and Richard Loving, who were sentenced under a Virginia statute that made their marriage illegal because she was black and he was white. Wadlington begins by discussing an older case,* Naim v. Naim, *that tested the constitutionality of those laws. He explains briefly the issue in* Loving v. Virginia *before considering the arguments in support of the constitutionality of miscegenation laws—the "nondiscrimination" argument, the legislative history argument, and the "reserved powers" argument. He also analyzes in detail the two main arguments against their constitutionality, which eventually would be cited by the Supreme Court—the due process argument and the equal protection argument.*

Walter Wadlington, "Virginia's Antimiscegnation Statute in Historical Perspective," *Virginia Law Review*, vol. 52, November 1966. Reproduced by permission.

N*aim v. Naim*, the first major test of the constitutionality of Virginia's miscegenation laws after their amendment in 1924, first reached the Supreme Court of Appeals in 1955. The case was not a criminal prosecution, but a suit for annulment. The plaintiff wife was white and her husband, according to the facts found by the court, was Chinese. The plaintiff was domiciled in Virginia when she and the defendant left the state to be married in North Carolina, which had no ban on such an interracial union. The parties returned to live in Virginia as husband and wife. Although the court found that the defendant was not a resident of Virginia at the time of the marriage, the defendant conceded that he and the plaintiff had left Virginia for the express purpose of evading its ban on interracial marriage.

In sustaining the lower court's annulment decree, the Supreme Court of Appeals specifically upheld the validity of the present miscegenation legislation. Replying to the key constitutional attacks based on the due process and equal protection clauses of the Fourteenth Amendment, the court said that regulation of marriage falls exclusively within the reserved powers of the states. Although the court did indicate that an attack might successfully be made on a miscegenation statute if its classification were arbitrary, it pointed out that since no evidence of unreasonableness appeared in the record, the classification by the legislature would be accorded a strong presumption of validity once it was determined that the purpose of the law was within the purview of state regulation and that the statute bore a reasonable relation to that purpose.

An appeal was taken to the United States Supreme Court, which in a per curiam ["by the Court as a whole"] decision vacated the Virginia court's judgment and remanded the case because of the record's inadequacy "as to the relationship of the parties to the Commonwealth of Virginia at the time of the marriage in North Carolina and upon their return to Virginia. . . ." The Court justified its action on the ground that the constitutional issue was not presented "in clean-cut and concrete form, unclouded" by other problems not clearly appearing but possibly relevant to the disposition of the case. However, the Virginia Supreme Court of Appeals restated on remand what it considered to be the material facts and said that they were sufficient for the annulment ruling under Virginia law. The court then noted that not only was there no Virginia procedure under which the record could be sent back to the trial court for supplementation under the circumstances, but that such a remand would in fact be contrary to existing practice and procedural rules. The court then reaffirmed its original decision upholding the annulment.

When the case reached the United States Supreme Court for the second time, the Virginia court's decision in response to the first order was noted, and the case was dismissed as "devoid of a properly presented federal question."

Much speculation about the meaning of the final dismissal of *Naim* by the Supreme Court has appeared in various legal publications. The Court's original remand seems to have been based upon the view that the application of Virginia's evasion statute to a person who was a nonresident at the time of the suit presented a distinct problem. However, whatever the grounds for the Supreme Court's dismissal may have been, as far as Virginia courts are concerned *Naim* appears to stand for three basic propositions. The first and most obvious of these is that the banning of interracial marriage is not unconstitutional unless the method of classification is arbitrary. Another is that in annulment suits at least the domiciliary connection of only one of the parties with Virginia at the time of the marriage is a sufficient basis for the application of the evasion statute. The third is that the 1924 act bans the marriage of a white with an Oriental as well as with a Negro.

Several years after the *Naim* case had completed its circuitous route through the courts, another case arose which challenged the constitutionality of a miscegenation ban upon the marriage between a white woman and a Filipino man. This was *Calma v. Calma*, . . . which ended with a procedural history almost as complicated as that of *Naim*. Because of the manner in which the case finally reached the Supreme Court of Appeals, however, that court found it unnecessary to consider the constitutional validity of the statute, and no appeal was taken to the United States Supreme Court from the decision.

This was the situation which existed when *Loving v. Commonwealth [of Virginia]*, long dormant because the parties had been living outside of Virginia in accordance with a judicial mandate, reached the appellate tribunals.

The Loving Case

In 1959 Richard and Mildred Loving were convicted, on guilty pleas, of the several-step offense of leaving Virginia to evade its miscegenation laws, marrying in the District of Columbia, and returning to Virginia and cohabiting as man and wife. According to the indictment, the husband was white and the wife was colored. Each party was sentenced to a year in jail, but both sentences were suspended "for a period of twenty-five years upon the provision that both accused leave . . . the state of Virginia at once and do not return together or at the same time . . . for a period of twenty-five years."

In late 1963 the Lovings filed a motion which sought to vacate the judgment against them and to have their sentences set aside on the grounds that the statute under which they were convicted was unconstitutional and that the sentences themselves were invalid. This motion was denied in early 1965, and the case then went to the Supreme Court of Appeals on writ of error. In March 1966 that court again declared the miscegenation statute to be constitutional, this time in a criminal case. Relying heavily on its earlier decision in *Naim*, the court pointed out that in the interim there had been no further decision "reflecting adversely on the validity of such statutes." The court also refused to accept the argument that the conditions attached to the suspension of the defendants' sentences were in effect a form of banishment, but did declare them to be "so unreasonable as to render the sentences void." Stating that only the cohabitation of the parties in Virginia—and not their returning to the state either singly or together—is prohibited by the statute, the court remanded the case for an amendment to the sentence consistent with its opinion.

Although it was disappointing to those who believe that the miscegenation laws are violative of fundamental civil liberties, the decision of the Supreme Court of Appeals was neither novel nor surprising. It should not have been expected that the court would overrule its decision in *Naim*, which was rendered little more than a decade [earlier] on federal constitutional grounds when the United States Supreme Court had been unable to find in *Naim* a clearly presented federal question on what appeared to be a very clear and complete statement of facts. On the other hand, the . . . decade [had] seen sweeping legal changes in the civil liberties field generally and in the field of race relations in particular—changes so sweeping in fact that the miscegenation statutes found in seventeen states [in 1966] constitute the last major category of legally enforced discrimination based solely on race. . . .

The Arguments Supporting the Constitutionality of Miscegenation Laws

The three principal arguments which have been advanced most frequently in support of the constitutionality of statutes prohibiting miscegenous marriages are: (1) the statutes are not discriminatory because they apply equally to members of each race affected by them; (2) historical debate in connection with the introduction of the Fourteenth Amendment in Congress indicates that elimination of the prohibition of interracial marriage was not part of the framers' intent; and (3) under the Tenth Amendment the regulation of marriage is exclusively within the province of the states.

The "Nondiscrimination" Argument

The proposition that if both parties to an interracial marriage are punishable equally there is no discrimination and hence no violation of the Fourteenth Amendment stems from the Supreme Court decision in *Pace v. Alabama*, which directly involved a statute prohibiting miscegenous cohabitation. Although many constitutional scholars have long considered *Pace* repudiated by more recent cases involving racial discrimination, it has nevertheless been the leading authority cited in many of the state court decisions upholding the validity of miscegenetic marriage prohibitions. In *McLaughlin* [*v. Florida*] it provided the basis for the decision of the Florida Supreme Court affirming the constitutionality of the state's statute prohibiting interracial cohabitation. Thus, although the majority of the United States Supreme Court found it unnecessary to take the step of ruling on miscegenous marriage statutes when *McLaughlin* came before them, they eliminated one of the key grounds on which state courts had previously relied to uphold interracial marriage bans by delivering the coup de grace to the *Pace* rationale.

The Legislative History Argument

The argument that some (and perhaps many) of those who voted for the passage of the Fourteenth Amendment did not intend that it should apply to state proscriptions against interracial marriage is discussed in great detail . . . in other publications. The fallacy of this argument is that it concentrates on only one of the factors which is relevant to constitutional interpretation. The genius of our Constitution lies in its capability to respond to social and economic change while preserving the continuity of the values which we inherit from the past. Although an analysis of the intentions of the framers of the document is proper in explaining the historical setting from which the Constitution and its amendments are derived, it must be recognized that the limitations of outlook which men of all historical periods share may preclude them from seeing the implications of the values which they enunciate. To the extent that succeeding generations find a fuller meaning in the ideals which the language of their forefathers expresses, and rely upon that language in developing their own senses of value, the law must provide them with the freedom to apply the words of the Constitution in a manner consonant with their own understanding.

The "Reserved Powers" Argument

The proposition that regulation of marriage should be left to the states has long been asserted by both state and federal courts in a number of contexts. Probably the leading federal authority is the 1888 United States Supreme Court case of *Maynard v. Hill*, which contained the famous dictum that "marriage, as creating the most important relation in life, as having more to do with the morals and civilization of a people than any other institution, has always been subject to control of the legislature." Today the regulation of marriage is regarded by some as the last great bulwark of States' rights. Concern is expressed that if the federal constitution can be construed to forbid the states from proscribing interracial marriage, it can also be interpreted to strike down other state regulations on the ground that they involve arbitrary classifications. Thus, it is argued, laws prohibiting marriage between parties related only by affinity or the marriage of epileptics may be held unconstitutional if miscegenation statutes are invalidated. Actually such an argument should be self-defeating if considered solely on a policy basis, because the past practice of leaving the regulation of marriage exclusively within the regulation of the states has led to a morass of conflicting and often anachronistic state legislation which has done more to tear down than to build up this "most important relation in life."

From a constitutional standpoint the question is not whether state marriage regulation has been preempted by federal law, but simply whether state power with regard to the regulation of marriage is subject to limitations established elsewhere in the Constitution. Accordingly, it would not follow from a Supreme Court holding that miscegenous marriage proscriptions are invalid that marriage is no longer predominantly subject to state regulation.

The Arguments Against the Constitutionality of Miscegenation Laws

Attacks on the constitutionality of miscegenation statutes generally have been grounded on the due process and equal protection clauses of the Fourteenth Amendment. . . .

The Due Process Argument

It is an axiom of federalism that the due process guarantees of the Fourteenth Amendment can be invoked only where there has been an infringement of some fundamental right. Thus the validity of miscegenation laws under the due process clause must turn in the first instance on the question whether marriage can be considered a fundamental right under the federal constitution. Although the language of *Maynard v. Hill* indicated the great importance accorded to marriage in our society, the Court did not speak of marriage in terms of a right. However, marriage was specifically so characterized in 1923 in the majority opinion in *Meyer v. Nebraska*. Moreover, in *Skinner v. Oklahoma*, a case involving compulsory sterilization of certain convicted criminals, the majority opinion stated that: "We are dealing here with legislation which involves one of the basic civil rights of man. Marriage and procreation are fundamental to the very existence and survival of the race."

The Right of Marital Privacy

This recognition of marriage as a right was reaffirmed in 1965 in *Griswold v. Connecticut*, which invalidated a state statute prohibiting the use of contraceptives. The Court said that the Connecticut law violated a fundamental right of marital privacy emanating from the First Amendment. To establish the existence of this right, a majority of the Justices—in several opinions—relied heavily on either *Meyer* or *Skinner* (or both) to support the proposition that marriage itself is a fundamental right. Moreover, Mr. Justice Douglas' opinion for the Court enunciated a basic right of association, which, it would seem, could be deemed equally relevant to a consideration of the validity of a statute which prohibits marriage across racial lines.

The establishment of marriage as a right is of course only the first step in determining whether miscegenation laws violate the due process clause. It must next be asked whether such laws unconstitutionally infringe this right, for it cannot be seriously contended that the right of marriage is absolute and cannot be infringed under any circumstances. A valid exercise of the state's police power can restrict that right. For example, it seems unlikely that a law prohibiting blood brothers and sisters from intermarrying could be successfully challenged under the due process clause (at least unless the evidence relating to the defective nature of the offspring of incestuous unions should be radically undermined). Similarly, a statute like the one held valid in *Buck v. Bell*, providing for the sterilization of certain mental defectives, does not seem open to constitutional attack, even though it invades the right to procreate through marriage announced by *Skinner v. Oklahoma*. Thus the question becomes whether the enactment of a miscegenation statute is a legitimate exercise of the state's police power in pursuit of a valid state objective.

Preservation of Racial Purity

If the state should contend that the purpose which its miscegenation law is designed to effectuate is simply the preservation of "racial pride," it seems clear that the enactment of the law is not within the scope of the state's police power. However, it is more likely that the state would contend that the purpose of the statute is to protect against a "corruption of blood" which would "weaken or destroy the quality of its citizenship." This contention would not render a miscegenation law impervious to constitutional attack. [S]tudies have seriously discredited the theory that a person of mixed blood is "inferior" in quality to one of absolute racial purity and is thus less capable of meeting the responsibilities of citizenship. Since state legislation is invalid under the due process clause unless it bears a reasonable relationship to its recited purpose and since courts cannot blind themselves to scientific evidence in passing upon the reasonableness of this relationship, these studies in themselves present a severe challenge to miscegenation laws. Moreover, even if it were assumed that the children of interracial marriages were not of as high a quality as those of racially pure marriages, miscegenation laws would still not be immune from constitutional attack. Although assuring the mental and physical well-being of its citizens is no doubt a valid state interest, there is a clear distinction between protecting against the generation of fundamentally defective offspring, as the statute upheld in *Buck v. Bell* was designed to do, and attempting to prevent by legislative enactment the birth of children who, though healthy, possess characteristics which, upon a subjective standard, may be less than ideal.

Do Miscegenation Laws Prevent Undue "Harm"?

Furthermore, where a right protected by the Constitution is invaded by state legislation, the courts have a responsibility to weigh several factors in determining whether this invasion is constitutionally justifiable. They must consider the nature of the harm which the questioned legislation seeks to combat and the probability that the harm will occur in the absence of the legislation, and balance these factors against the severity of the restriction on individual freedom. It is doubtful that a miscegenation law, particularly Virginia's, could stand under such a balancing test. Evidence produced by sociological, biological, and anthropological studies is as relevant to an inquiry into the nature of the harm sought to be curtailed by miscegenation laws as it is in determining the reasonableness of the relationship between those laws and their recited purpose. Moreover, even if a court did not find these studies to be conclusive, but merely sufficient to shed doubt on the theory that offspring of interracial unions are inferior, it might well invalidate a miscegenation law on the ground that the existence of a hypothetical harm does not justify a drastic invasion of individual liberty. A miscegenation law may put an individual to a cruel choice between marrying the person whom he loves and leaving his home, or denying his affections and remaining in the state. The probability that the law will force an individual to choose between these highly unsatisfactory alternatives is especially great in Virginia because the classifications upon which her miscegenation laws operate are so broad.

The Equal Protection Argument

An analysis of the equal protection argument which can be leveled against miscegenation laws must begin with an examination of the recent Supreme Court case of *McLaughlin v. Florida*. For although the Court specifically refused to reach the question of the constitutionality of Florida's miscegenation law in striking down an interracial cohabitation statute, it did provide the basis upon which an equal protection attack on miscegenation laws should proceed.

The challenged statute in *McLaughlin* specified a punishment for "any negro man and white woman, or any white man and negro woman, who are not married to each other, who shall habitually live in and occupy in the nighttime the same room." This statute was supplementary to other general statutes proscribing lewd cohabitation and fornication, and was distinguishable from them only in that it (1) applied only to interracial couples, and (2) did not require proof of intercourse as an element of the crime. The Supreme Court held that the statute violated the equal protection clause of the Fourteenth Amendment. The Court reasoned that unless an "overriding statutory purpose" could be found justifying the punishment of a white person and a Negro for conduct which was not punished when engaged in by any other persons, "the racial classification contained in . . . [the statute] is reduced to an invidious discrimination forbidden by the Equal Protection Clause."

"Sexual Decency" and Racial Cohabitation

Florida first contended that such a purpose could be founded upon the state's interest in preventing "breaches of the basic concept of sexual decency." Although it is clear that this is a valid state interest justifying the exercise of the police power, it is equally clear that this interest could not justify the discriminatory classification found in the cohabitation statute because, as the Court pointed out, there was no suggestion made that an interracial couple is more likely to occupy the same room together—or to engage in sexual intercourse if they do—than an intraracial couple.

Florida's next contention was that the cohabitation statute was ancillary to, and designed to accomplish the same purpose as, the state's miscegenation statute which was itself constitutional. The Court answered this contention without considering the validity of the miscegenation law, on the ground that a statute which involves "invidious official discrimination based on race . . . will be upheld only if it is necessary, and not merely rationally related, to the accomplishment of a permissible state policy." The Court reasoned that Florida had not demonstrated that the interracial cohabitation statute was necessary to accomplish the purpose of the miscegenation law, since it punished only extra-marital conduct, which could be reached by the general statutory provisions proscribing fornication and lewd cohabitation.

Since Virginia has statutes proscribing fornication and lewd and lascivious cohabitation and since these statutes might in theory be invoked to punish a party to a miscegenous marriage on the ground that a separate statutory provision renders miscegenous marriages void, it could be argued that *McLaughlin* has already invalidated the Virginia miscegenation law because these statutes make the criminal ban against interracial marriage "unnecessary." This argument might seem to draw support from the Virginia court's assertion in *Loving* that "the real gravamen [grounds for legal action] of the offense charged against the defendants . . . was their *cohabitation as man and wife*," which arguably suggests that the conduct of the Lovings could have been punished equally effectively under the lascivious cohabitation statute. However, the only reason that the court considered cohabitation to be the critical element of the offense in *Loving* was that the parties were prosecuted under Section 20–58 of the Virginia Code, the evasion provision of the miscegenation law, which depends upon cohabitation within the state to establish the state contact necessary for prosecution. Section 20–58 is clearly ancillary to—and in fact derives its criminal sanction from—section 20–59, which punishes the interracial marriage itself. Accordingly, it was their cohabitation *as man and wife* which was said to be the gravamen of the Lovings' offense. Thus it is apparent that the Virginia miscegenation provisions are designed to punish the act of interracial marriage itself and—where necessary to establish sufficient state contact—interracial *marital* cohabitation, rather than fornication or illicit cohabitation in general. On the other hand, the conduct punished by the statute in question in *McLaughlin* was extramarital interracial cohabitation. Therefore, *McLaughlin* does not provide authority for the proposition that Virginia's miscegenation provisions are rendered unnecessary by her fornication and lewd and lascivious cohabitation statutes.

Miscegenation Lacks Statutory Purpose

At another level, however, the contention that Virginia's miscegenation law is "unnecessary" may well prove fatal to the constitutionality of that law under the equal protection clause. The Court's analysis in *McLaughlin* suggests a dual inquiry. First, it must be asked whether there is an "overriding statutory purpose" which justifies the discrimination in the questioned statute. Second, if a permissible state purpose is found, it must then be asked if the racially drawn statute is *necessarily* related to the accomplishment of this policy. A negative answer to either of these questions will invalidate the law. Thus Virginia appears poised on the horns of a dilemma in attempting to justify her miscegenation law. If she should argue that the policy which the law is designed to accomplish is simply the preservation of racial purity, she could easily demonstrate that statutory provisions punishing interracial marriage are necessary to the accomplishment of this purpose. However, it is unlikely that the preservation of racial purity in itself can be considered a permissible state purpose justifying the repressive exercise of the police power. That at least two members of the Court would not find an "overriding statutory purpose"—however articulated—justifying a miscegenation law seems to be foreshadowed by the language of Mr. Justice [Potter] Stewart, joined by Mr. Justice [William O.] Douglas, concurring in *McLaughlin*: "I cannot conceive of a valid legislative purpose under our Constitution for a state law which makes the color of a person's skin the test of whether his conduct is a criminal offense." On the other hand, if Virginia should argue that the policy which the miscegenation law is designed to accomplish is the protection against the birth of "inferior" (in an objective sense) offspring—which may be a permissible state purpose—she would then have to prove that the miscegenation law is *necessary* to the accomplishment of this purpose. This would inevitably involve proof of the "inferiority" of children of "interracial" unions, an awkward burden in the second half of the twentieth century.

The Virginia miscegenation law appears to be invalid under the equal protection clause on still another ground. Although entitled "An Act to Preserve Racial Integrity," the statute in fact seeks to preserve only the integrity of one race, the Caucasian. Thus, although whites are precluded from marrying nonwhites (subject to the Pocahontas exception), Orientals may marry Negroes, Melanesians may marry Negritos, and any number of other combinations may be joined conjugally. This distinction renders the statute's classification arbitrary and unreasonable in light of its ostensible factual premise, asserted by the Virginia Supreme Court of Appeals, that "nations and races have better advanced in human progress when they cultivated their own distinctive characteristics and culture and developed their own peculiar genius." Furthermore, the prohibition against Caucasians marrying anyone with any "trace whatever of any blood other than Caucasian" itself appears to be arbitrary and unreasonable even if it is assumed that persons with differing racial characteristics should be precluded from intermarrying.

> "Loving *was not only more united in its judgment, but in its analysis as well, more than it has been in any other marriage case in this century.*"

The Right to Marry Is Socially, Personally, and Constitutionally Important

Lynn D. Wardle

Lynn D. Wardle is a professor of law at Brigham Young University. In the following viewpoint, he offers an analysis of the Court's decision in Loving v. Virginia, *focusing on the brief discussion in the written opinion on the right to marry. The case, as he explains, involved a Virginia couple, Mildred Jeter, a black woman, and Richard Loving, a white man, who were required to leave Virginia or face a jail sentence because their marriage under Virginia's miscegenation laws was illegal. The Supreme Court found that those laws were unconstitutional. Wardle explains that the Supreme Court's opinion focused on three elements in the Virginia statue: (1) that the law used a suspect method of classification (race); (2) that its purpose was suspect (to uphold policy that whites were superior to blacks); and (3) that it restricted a preferentially protected relationship (marriage). Wardle also says that the very brief discussion of the freedom to marry in the written opinion is remarkable for a number of reasons: it is legally binding and not mere* dicta, *or explanation of the judges' views; the justices were united in their decision and analysis; it was written by the Chief Justice; it invalidated a*

Lynn D. Wardle, "*Loving v. Virginia* and the Constitutional Right to Marry, 1790–1990," *Howard Law Journal*, Symposium: Law and the Politics of Marriage; *Loving v. Virginia* After Thirty Years, vol. 41, no. 2, Winter 1998, pp. 289–347. Reproduced by permission.

marriage law; it came at a time when the country was involved in various issues regarding segregation; it used little precedent in coming to its conclusion; and it was written with a directness that underscored the confidence of the judges' decision.

In *Loving v. Virginia,* the Supreme Court invalidated a Virginia law that prohibited interracial marriages. . . . For purposes of understanding the discussion of the "right to marry," the salient facts may be summarized briefly, as follows. Richard Perry Loving, a white man, and Mildred Jeter, a part-Negro and part-Indian woman, were lawfully married in the District of Columbia in June of 1958. They returned to Virginia to live and within months were charged with violating Virginia's anti-miscegenation statute, a crime that carried a penalty of one to five years imprisonment. In January 1959, they pled guilty and were sentenced by an expressly racist judge to a year in jail, with the sentence suspended on the condition that they leave the State and not return for 25 years. As a result, the Lovings moved to the District of Columbia. Almost five years later the Lovings filed a motion in the Virginia court to vacate the judgment and set aside the sentence, on the ground that the statutes which they violated were unconstitutional under the Fourteenth Amendment. More than a year later, the state court denied the motion, and the Lovings appealed to the Supreme Court of Appeals of Virginia, which likewise, upheld the constitutionality of the anti-miscegenation statutes. The convictions were affirmed, but the sentences were modified. The Lovings sought review in the Supreme Court of the United States which unanimously reversed.

The opinion of the Court, written by Chief Justice Warren, was relatively short, only 12 pages. All of the justices unanimously joined in the judgment, with eight justices joining the Court's opinion. In addition, one brief concurring opinion was written, essentially agreeing with the main racial equality principle of the Court's opinion.

The Court's Opinion

The Court opinion focused on three fundamental elements in the Virginia anti-miscegenation statute: (1) the law used a suspect method of classification (race); (2) to achieve a suspect purpose (to maintain an official public policy that the White race is superior and the Black race inferior); and, (3) did so by restricting a preferentially protected relationship (marriage). The bulk of the opinion focuses on the first two elements, the undeniable fact that the law constituted "invidious racial discrimination . . . designed to maintain White Supremacy." As Professor Cass R. Sunstein described it:

> The key sentence in *Loving* says that "the racial classifications [at issue] must stand on their own justification, as measures designed to maintain White Supremacy." This striking reference to White Supremacy—by a unanimous Court, capitalizing both words and speaking in these terms for the only time in the nation's history—was designed to get at the core of Virginia's argument that discrimination on the basis of participation in mixed marriages was not discrimination on the basis of race. . . . Viewed in context—in light of its actual motivations and its actual effects—the ban was thus part of a system of racial caste.

In no uncertain terms, the Court condemned and struck down the racist scheme and purpose of the Virginia anti-miscegenation law.

The Right to Marry

At the end of the opinion, the Court briefly turned to the third point—the fact that the law restricted the socially, personally and Constitutionally important relationship of *marriage*. The "right-to-marry" part of the opinion was extremely short, only two paragraphs, placed at the very end of the opinion:

> These statutes also deprive the Lovings of liberty without due process of law in violation of the Due Process Clause of

the Fourteenth Amendment. The freedom to marry has long been recognized as one of the vital personal rights essential to the orderly pursuit of happiness by free men.

Marriage is one of the 'basic civil rights of man,' fundamental to our very existence and survival. To deny this fundamental freedom on so unsupportable a basis as the racial classifications embodied in these statutes, classifications so directly subversive of the principle of equality at the heart of the Fourteenth Amendment, is surely to deprive all the State's citizens of liberty without due process of law. The Fourteenth Amendment requires that the freedom of choice to marry not be restricted by invidious racial discriminations. Under our Constitution, the freedom to marry or not marry, a person of another race resides with the individual and cannot be infringed by the State.

In these brief sentences, the *Loving* Court makes four important points about the constitutional right to marry. First, "the freedom to marry" is protected by the Due Process Clause of the Fourteenth Amendment. Second, the "right to marry" is given special Constitutional protection because it traditionally has been deemed special, "has long been recognized," and because it is "essential to the orderly pursuit of happiness by free men." Third, to allow a state to deny such a "basic," "fundamental" right on the basis of "invidious racial discrimination" subverts the very foundation of liberty from an equal rights perspective. Fourth, "the freedom to marry . . . a person of another race" constitutionally may not be restricted by the State. Thus, *Loving* clearly established the parameters of the right to marry (historically established and essential to ordered liberty), its constitutional shelter (the Fourteenth Amendment), and its practical importance to society (the foundation of liberty). *Loving* also underscored the Court's substantial deference to state marriage regulation, emphasizing the extraordinary nature of Virginia's racist marriage restriction that so blatantly defied the Fourteenth Amendment that the Court was compelled to invalidate it.

The Right as Legally Binding

The brief discussion of the freedom to marry in *Loving* is remarkable for many reasons. First, it is legally binding, not mere *dicta*. The Virginia statute under review directly regulated marriage, and the Court's analysis of the right to marry is an integral part of the opinion. *Loving* was the first Supreme Court case in more than 175 years to directly pass on the constitutional validity of a marriage law. (The Court in *Reynolds* [*v. United States*] had reviewed a federal law proscribing polygamy in the territories, but the immediate issue was whether a defendant could raise a First Amendment defense to prosecution for violation of a federal law—regardless of the subject of the federal law.)

The Unanimity and Harmony of the Decision

Second, the Supreme Court in *Loving* was not only more united in its judgment, but in its analysis as well, more than it has been in any other marriage case in this century. The judgment of the Court in *Loving* was unanimous, and eight of the justices joined in the "right-to-marry analysis." (Justice Stewart concurred in the judgment upon the basis of the racial equality analysis only.) The *Loving* Court undeniably was more harmonious than it has been in the thirty years since then, and arguably more united than in any of the prior marriage cases—except, nominally, in the *Reynolds* case nearly a century earlier, and arguably the true disposition of the Court was more united in *Loving* than in *Reynolds*. *Loving* was a unanimous decision and only two opinions—with no dissenting opinion. Contrast *Loving* with *Zablocki v. Redhail*, decided only 11 years later by a severely split Court that produced 6 opinions, including strong dissenting opinions, and *Turner v. Safley*, a case decided two decades after *Loving*, that produced a nominally unanimous judgment, but a severe 5-4 split (on some issues) and two very divergent opinions, with four justices signing the dissenting-in-part opinion.

The Decision Authored by the Chief Justice

Third, the opinion in *Loving* was written by the Chief Justice, a fact of importance, in that it sent a particularly strong and credible message. The last, and only other, Supreme Court case discussing the right to marry in which the opinion for the Court was written by the Chief Justice as *Reynolds*—decided nearly a century earlier—which put an end to polygamous marriage. No marriage case decided since *Loving* has been authored by the Chief Justice.

Invalidation of a Marriage Law

Fourth, *Loving* was the first case in which the Supreme Court invalidated a marriage law. It previously had overturned what it considered an erroneous interpretation of a marriage law nearly a century earlier, but had previously not struck down a marriage law in any significant case. Given the tremendous deference shown the state legislatures, and the long-established emphasis on the ultimate responsibility of the states to regulate marriage in our federal system, *Loving* was a profound break with precedent.

The Timing of the Decision

Fifth, the timing of the decision invalidating anti-miscegenation laws is noteworthy. In the previous fifteen years, the Court could have addressed the issue of whether laws forbidding interracial marriages violated a constitutional "right to marry" in three separate cases, but it chose to avoid ruling on the issue. The Court might have chosen segregated marriage instead of segregated education as the setting for the main case in which to constitutionally repudiate segregation. Perhaps the Court waited so long after *Brown v. Board of Education*, thirteen years, to remedy the evil of anti-miscegenation laws because of prudential considerations that the effort to overturn centuries of government-sponsored invidious racial discrimination could not be pressed too quickly. Those who objected to integrated education might have resisted even more vigorously, more passionately, more *violently*, if their fears of the mixing of the races among hormone-awakening, romantically-inclined older adolescents in high school, had been combined with fears of interracial marriage.

The Brevity of the Discussion of the Right to Marry

The sixth point of importance is the brevity of the discussion of the constitutional right to marry in *Loving* and the Court's scarce use of precedent. For instance, the Supreme Court made no reference to its prior marriage decision, *Reynolds v. United States*. Neither did the Court cite its strong *dicta* about marriage in its ruling two years earlier in *Griswold v. Connecticut*. The Court did not discuss any other marriage cases. Rather, the Court simply cited only two cases, *Skinner v. Oklahoma*, and *Maynard v. Hill*. *Skinner* is a direct citation as authority for the proposition that marriage is a basic civil right; *Maynard* is merely a "see also" cite. Perhaps the reason for this lack of citation was to keep the Court's focus clean and its point clear. The Court did not wish to clutter the issue with debate over the use of contraceptives or the revival of substantive due process (*Griswold*), or open a can of worms concerning the limits on the government's authority to regulate marriage in ways that infringe upon the free exercise of religion (*Reynolds*)—a fundamental freedom which, like the right to be free from governmental racial discrimination, has a textual basis that is explicitly rooted in the amendments to the Constitution. The Court did want to make the point that the fundamental importance of marriage to individuals and to society had long been recognized by the Court and to link the importance of marriage to procreation, so it cited—but merely cited—two old cases to confirm those points (*Maynard* and *Skinner*).

The brevity of the discussion of the right to marry in *Loving* is further enhanced because no treatises, professors, or other experts are cited. The abundant literature dealing with the right to marry and a half-dozen major cases that previously mentioned it, were entirely ignored. The Court apparently did not think that it needed the external support of academic commentators to validate or support the point it was making; that a consenting man and woman of different races, otherwise eligible to marry, have a fundamental constitutional right to marry each other. Perhaps it did not want to dilute the unpoliticized integrity of that point by citing legal commentators who discussed the right to marry in the context of advocating various constitutional theories, each associated with an ideological agenda.

A Confident Decision

The brevity and conciseness of the discussion of the constitutional right to marry in *Loving* also indicates that the Court was confident about its judgment, and believed that it did not need extensive rhetorical justification. The Court was right, and believed it could explain very clearly why it was right in just a few words. Perhaps it knew that a concise explanation would persuade most reasonable Americans that it was right, and a longer explanation would not persuade those who disagreed, and detailed social policy justification might produce interpretive mischief that could come back to haunt the Court. The Court in *Loving* had no need to rhetorically "sell" either its judgment or its succinct right-to-marry analysis. It stood securely on its own merits. By contrast, in many cases wherein the Court appears less confident in its judgment, and less unified, it seems that the Justices feel compelled to write long, passionate, exaggerated opinions to compensate for the lack of real consensus and confidence.

"I believe all Americans, no matter their race, no matter their sex, no matter their sexual orientation, should have that same freedom to marry."

The Right to Marry Should Extend to All

Mildred Loving

Mildred Loving was a black woman who married a white man in Virginia, in violation of the Racial Integrity Act, which prohibited a white person from marrying outside his or her race. Loving and her husband, Richard, took their case to the Supreme Court, which struck down interracial marriage bans in the 1967 Loving v. Virginia *decision. On June 12, 2007, forty years after the announcement of the Supreme Court decision, Mildred Loving released a public statement regarding the case and her views on marriage. She explains that her husband fought their famous court case not for a "cause," but because of their love for each other. She expresses her gratitude to those who helped them in their struggle, and is heartened at how the case changed the way people think about race and marriage in this country. Loving says she believes that all couples, no matter their sexual orientation, should enjoy the same freedom to marry that she and her husband were finally granted.*

When my late husband, Richard, and I got married in Washington, D.C., in 1958, it wasn't to make a political statement or start a fight. We were in love, and we wanted to be married.

Mildred Loving, "Loving for All," Freedomtomarry.org, June 12, 2007. Reproduced by permission.

We didn't get married in Washington because we wanted to marry there. We did it there because the government wouldn't allow us to marry back home in Virginia where we grew up, where we met, where we fell in love, and where we wanted to be together and build our family. You see, I am a woman of color and Richard was white, and at that time people believed it was okay to keep us from marrying because of their ideas of who should marry whom.

When Richard and I came back to our home in Virginia, happily married, we had no intention of battling over the law. We made a commitment to each other in our love and lives, and now had the legal commitment, called marriage, to match. Isn't that what marriage is?

Our Arrest and Prosecution

Not long after our wedding, we were awakened in the middle of the night in our own bedroom by deputy sheriffs and actually arrested for the "crime" of marrying the wrong kind of person. Our marriage certificate was hanging on the wall above the bed.

The state prosecuted Richard and me, and after we were found guilty, the judge declared: "Almighty God created the races white, black, yellow, Malay and red, and he placed them on separate continents. And but for the interference with his arrangement there would be no cause for such marriages. The fact that he separated the races shows that he did not intend for the races to mix." He sentenced us to a year in prison, but offered to suspend the sentence if we left our home in Virginia for 25 years exile.

Fighting for Love, Not a Cause

We left, and got a lawyer. Richard and I had to fight, but still were not fighting for a cause. We were fighting for our love.

Though it turned out we had to fight, happily Richard and I didn't have to fight alone. Thanks to groups like the ACLU

[American Civil Liberties Union] and the NAACP [National Association for the Advancement of Colored People] Legal Defense & Education Fund, and so many good people around the country willing to speak up, we took our case for the freedom to marry all the way to the U.S. Supreme Court. And on June 12, 1967, the Supreme Court ruled unanimously that, "The freedom to marry has long been recognized as one of the vital personal rights essential to the orderly pursuit of happiness by free men," a "basic civil right."

My generation was bitterly divided over something that should have been so clear and right. The majority believed that what the judge said, that it was God's plan to keep people apart, and that government should discriminate against people in love. But I have lived long enough now to see big changes. The older generation's fears and prejudices have given way, and today's young people realize that if someone loves someone they have a right to marry.

The Freedom to Marry for All

Surrounded as I am now by wonderful children and grandchildren, not a day goes by that I don't think of Richard and our love, our right to marry, and how much it meant to me to have that freedom to marry the person precious to me, even if others thought he was the "wrong kind of person" for me to marry. I believe all Americans, no matter their race, no matter their sex, no matter their sexual orientation, should have that same freedom to marry. Government has no business imposing some people's religious beliefs over others. Especially if it denies people's civil rights.

I am still not a political person, but I am proud that Richard's and my name is on a court case that can help reinforce the love, the commitment, the fairness, and the family that so many people, black or white, young or old, gay or straight seek in life. I support the freedom to marry for all. That's what *Loving*, and loving, are all about.

"*[The] ruling has been important to the development of a number of different constitutional doctrines, including the Constitution's protection for marriage, the proposition that there are constitutional limits on state regulation of domestic relations, and the proposition that racial classifications are invidious.*"

Loving's Landmark Case Status Is Well-Deserved

Joanna Grossman

Joanna Grossman is a professor of law at Hofstra University. In the following viewpoint, she discusses the cultural and legal legacy of the Loving v. Virginia *decision. The case involved an interracial couple, Mildred Jeter and Richard Loving, who were prohibited from living in Virginia—and faced jail time if they did so—because their marriage was found to be illegal under a Virginia statute that banned marriage between races. Grossman says that the immediate impact of the decision was to liberate the Lovings, so they could return from exile to their home of Virginia with their children. The cultural legacy of the decision is less certain; to this day, marriages between blacks and whites are rare, asserts Grossman. But the ruling has been important to the development of other constitutional doctrines, including the protection for marriage, the limits on state regulation of domestic relations, and the invidiousness of racial classifications. Grossman further explains that same-sex marriage advocates have in-*

Joanna Grossman, "The Fortieth Anniversary of *Loving v. Virginia*: The Legal Legacy of the Case That Ended Legal Prohibitions on Interracial Marriage, Parts I and II," Findlaw.com, May 30, 2007, and June 12, 2007. Reproduced by permission.

voked Loving to argue that a ban on same-sex marriage is a form of sex discrimination, just as a ban on interracial marriage is a form of race discrimination.

June 12, [2007] will mark the 40th anniversary of *Loving v. Virginia*, the 1967 opinion in which the U.S. Supreme Court ruled that Virginia's criminal ban on interracial marriage was unconstitutional.

The ruling sounded the death knell for anti-miscegenation laws not only in Virginia, but also in the fifteen other states that still had them on the books. In this column, I'll ask: What is the legacy of this opinion, four decades later?

The Case's Path to the Supreme Court

Loving v. Virginia was, ultimately, a case about one marriage: that of Mildred Jeter, a part-African, part-Cherokee woman, and Richard Loving, a white man, who crossed the border in 1958 from their home state of Virginia to neighboring Washington, D.C., to marry. After Jeter and Loving returned to Virginia and set up house, they were indicted for violating Virginia's ban on interracial marriages.

The indictment came about when three law enforcement officers entered the Lovings' bedroom, shined a flashlight on them, and demanded to know why Richard was in bed with "this lady". The officers were unimpressed by the D.C. marriage certificate hanging on the wall; "That's no good here," Richard was told. (The details of the arrest are described, among other places, in a 1992 *New York Times* article by David Margolick entitled "A Mixed Marriage.")

The Lovings were arrested and convicted pursuant to a Virginia law that criminalized not only marriage between a white person and a "colored person" in Virginia, but also such a marriage when entered into out of state, if the marriage was celebrated by Virginia residents who left in order to evade the state's prohibition.

The trial judge suspended the sentences, on the condition that the couple leave the state of Virginia and not return there together for twenty-five years. The judge infamously opined at sentencing that: "Almighty God created the races white, black, yellow, Malay and red, and he placed them on separate continents. And but for the interference with his arrangement there would be no cause for such marriages. The fact that he separated the races shows that he did not intend for the races to mix."

After being convicted in Virginia, the Lovings relocated to neighboring D.C., in order to comply with the conditions of their sentences. However, they returned to Virginia four years later to challenge their convictions as violating both the Equal Protection and Due Process Clauses of the Fourteenth Amendment of the U.S. Constitution.

The Lovings' Day in the Supreme Court

The Lovings took their case all the way to the U.S. Supreme Court. Their claim was a novel one, since, at that time, the Supreme Court had never invalidated a state restriction on marriage. The Court's role, instead, had been limited to refereeing conflicts between the states, which had long differed about what restrictions to place on eligibility for marriage and the accessibility of divorce. Before *Loving*, then, rather than developing federal law norms about the right approach to regulating marriage and divorce, the Court had needed only to develop a coherent approach to interstate conflicts. This limited role for federal courts was consistent with the long-standing belief that domestic relations law was an area reserved to the states.

Loving, however, heralded a new era for the Supreme Court—one in which the Court forced state marriage laws to yield to developing federal constitutional norms of equality and privacy. In striking down Virginia's anti-miscegenation law, the Supreme Court reached three important conclusions:

First, although earlier cases had implied that states' power to regulate marriage was unlimited, the Court in *Loving* made clear that state marriage laws must comply with federal constitutional norms.

Second, the Court concluded that Virginia's miscegenation ban violated the Equal Protection Clause of the Fourteenth Amendment, because it relied on a race-based classification to define eligibility to marry. Virginia had argued, unsuccessfully, that because its statutes "punish equally both the white and the Negro participants in an interracial marriage, these statutes, despite their reliance on racial classifications, do not constitute an invidious discrimination on the basis of race." The Court rejected this "equal application" theory of discrimination law, noting that the fact that the law "prohibits only interracial marriages involving white persons demonstrates that the classifications must stand on their own justification, as measures designed to maintain White Supremacy." Such a law, the Court concluded, violates the "central meaning of the Equal Protection Clause."

Third, and finally, the Court concluded that Virginia's miscegenation ban also violated the Due Process Clause of the Fourteenth Amendment. "The freedom to marry has long been recognized as one of the vital personal rights essential to the orderly pursuit of happiness by free men," the Court explained. "Marriage is one of the 'basic civil rights of man,' fundamental to our very existence and survival." Under the Court's substantive due process doctrine, fundamental rights cannot be infringed without a compelling governmental reason. Virginia had no such reason to justify its ban, and thus the Court found a clear Due Process violation.

The immediate import of *Loving* was clear: States no longer had the power to prohibit interracial marriages. However, as the next sections will explore, the ruling had other notable effects as well.

The Legacy of *Loving* for the Lovings Themselves

With the Supreme Court's ruling in hand, the Lovings were finally able to return to Virginia without fear of criminal persecution, and with the veil of illegitimacy raised from the heads of their three interracial children. That meant a great deal to them, for returning home as a couple was their ultimate goal, according to Robert Pratt, who knew both Richard and Mildred.

Interestingly, the Lovings did not see themselves as civil rights activists or heroes, but rather simply as people engaged in a personal struggle for freedom. They did not attend the argument in the Supreme Court, and, when asked by *Ebony* magazine what the ruling meant for them, Richard said only that: "For the first time, I could put my arm around her and publicly call her my wife." Mildred reported similar sentiments, telling the *Washington Post* in 1967 that "I feel free now . . . it was a great burden."

Though many people remained opposed to interracial marriage, the Lovings told reporters they had the support of their hometown community and were welcomed home. Richard told *Life* magazine that they "encounter hostile stares only when they venture away."

The Lovings' marriage ended tragically in 1975 when Richard was killed by a drunk driver. Mildred lost an eye in the same accident, but lived several decades more without Richard. She and the sheriff who arrested them never "exchanged a single word," though both lived in the same small Virginia town for decades.

When David Margolick interviewed the sheriff for the *New York Times* in honor of the 25th anniversary of the ruling, in 1992, the sheriff was unapologetic about his role in the case. He said, "I was acting according to the law at the time, and I still think it should be on the books. I don't think a white person should marry a black person. I'm from the old school. The Lord made sparrows and robins, not to mix with one another."

The Cultural Legacy of *Loving*

Occurring just two months after the Court handed down its *Loving* decision, Virginia's first interracial marriage was scarcely noted by the press. And months later, the first interracial marriage in Tennessee was celebrated on the steps of the Nashville City Hall and Courthouse.

Yet the acceptance of interracial marriage was by no means immediate nationwide. Indeed, the day after the decision came down, the sitting Governor of Georgia, Lester Maddox, observed that he would prefer to see "less mixed marriages. But if one doesn't know any better than to mess up, let them have it."

It is hard to say whether this view represented any kind of national consensus, but Maddox's begrudging acceptance of the legal ruling despite his clear objection to the underlying social practice was no doubt shared by others. Indeed, in a 1964 *New York Times* article, Anthony Lewis predicted that the invalidation of laws banning intimacy between whites and blacks would have little practical effect: "Only social disapproval really inhibits marriage between whites and Negroes now. Any southern couple desiring to marry in the face of a state anti-miscegenation law can go to a state without one. It is the whole social apparatus of caste, and history, that makes intermarriage unlikely."

Lewis's prediction was reinforced by an article a few years later in which Barry Furlong reported on several black-white interracial marriages in which the respondents described a variety of problems, both personal and societal, that resulted from their status as parties to a racially-mixed marriage. Furlong asserted that "[t]here is a singularity to each of those marriages, though some are more singular than others. No one couple reflects all of the woes and tribulations of marriages across racial lines, but there are some representative reactions and problems." The problems reported ranged from family estrangement, to rejection by religious groups, to difficulty traveling.

Yet despite these reports, there is no doubt that cultural opposition to interracial marriage diminished in the decades before and after *Loving.* Several religious authorities openly supported the practice. In 1963, for example, the National Catholic Welfare Conference adopted resolutions deploring "the attitudes and cruel behavior of American society which penalizes and ostracizes those persons who exercise their fundamental human right to free choice of a marital partner by entering into interracial marriages." The United Presbyterian Church wrote a position paper calling for the immediate repeal of all laws banning interracial marriage. Meanwhile, opposition within secular institutions also diminished. In 1963, for example, the United States Air Force ended its practice of asking personnel whether they had married a person of another race during their overseas tours.

However, cultural acceptance of interracial marriage was far from complete in the 1960s, and, even today, interracial marriage is relatively rare. As law professor Rachel Moran notes in her book, *Interracial Intimacy,* "[a]ntimiscegenation laws played a critical role in defining racial difference, enforcing racial inequality, and establishing the boundaries of proper sexual and marital practices. The *Loving* decision lifted formal restrictions on intermarriage, but it would be naive to think that the Court could instantly undo the informal assumptions and practices that developed during three centuries of a 'separate but equal' principle in sex, marriage, and family."

Research about patterns of racial intermarriage and racial preference in the selection of intimate partners confirms this conclusion. One recent study documented significant increases in interracial marriage since the 1970s, but also noted trends that reflect *Loving's* limits. Interracial marriages account for only 6 percent of all marriages in the United States, and African-Americans remain the "least likely of all racial/ethnic minorities to marry whites." The same study concluded that although "the pace of marital assimilation among African Americans proceeded more rapidly over the 1990s than it did in earlier decades, the social boundaries between African Americans and whites nevertheless remain highly rigid and resilient to change." Research on dating preferences also reveals that a significant proportion of the population still prefers to date people of their own race.

The cultural legacy of *Loving*, like the law's power to transform societal norms more generally, is thus limited.

Constructing a Legal Legacy

Loving v. Virginia obviously had immediate, liberating effects for Mildred and Richard Loving, who were able to return home with their children after several years living effectively in exile. And other couples residing in states like Virginia were similarly freed from the constraints of an outdated and discriminatory law.

But *Loving's* legacy extends beyond these immediate effects. While the ruling in *Loving* hastened the demise of bans on interracial marriage, such laws were already on their way out; fourteen states had repealed them without judicial pressure in the decades prior. The rest of these laws, too, would eventually have fallen as cultural norms evolved even further away from those of the era that embraced racial segregation and explicit subordination. But a landmark case like *Loving* should be remembered for its effects on other legal doctrines as well.

The Supreme Court in *Loving* invalidated Virginia's antimiscegenation law on two constitutional grounds: It held the law violated the Equal Protection Clause because race-based classifications are invidious, permissible only when justified by a compelling governmental purpose. In addition, it held that law violated the Due Process Clause because the right to marry "is one of the vital personal rights essential to the orderly pursuit of happiness by free men," one that is "fundamental to our very existence and survival."

Legally speaking, that ruling has been important to the development of a number of different constitutional doctrines, including the Constitution's protection for marriage, the proposition that there are constitutional limits on state regulation of domestic relations, and the proposition that racial classifications are invidious.

Constitutional Protection for the Right to Marry

Because *Loving* was so tied up with race, and the particular law the case invalidated was so clearly inspired by racism, it is not immediately clear what impact, if any, the ruling would have on the validity of other marriage restrictions. Was it only because Virginia's law defined the right to marry on the basis of race that it was constitutionally infirm?

Certainly, the ruling did not generally override state law with respect to marriage, nor did it signify that all marriage restrictions were equally invidious. Only a few years later, for example, the Supreme Court dismissed an appeal in *Baker v. Nelson*, one of the first cases to challenge the constitutionality of a state's ban on same-sex marriage, "for want of substantial federal question." It thus left the state bans on same-sex marriage intact, despite *Loving's* strong language about the fundamental importance of the right to marry.

The Court's next marriage case, however, solidified constitutional protection for marriage even in the absence of a racial classification. In *Zablocki v. Redhail*, a 1978 case, the Court struck down a Wisconsin statute prohibiting noncustodial parents who were behind on support obligations from marrying if their children were on welfare.

The Court began its analysis of the Wisconsin law by citing *Loving*—the "leading decision" on "the right to marry"—and used heightened scrutiny to evaluate the law, even though it involved no race-based or other suspect classification, simply because marriage is a right "of fundamental importance." *Zablocki* thus made clear that *Loving's* unwillingness to tolerate certain marriage restrictions was not limited to those drawn on the basis of race.

Loving and the Battle for Same-Sex Marriage

The Supreme Court has not revisited the right to marry in twenty years, but the law of marriage can hardly, today, be considered settled. The scope of the right to marry remains fiercely contested because of the issue of same-sex marriage, and *Loving* has played a central role in that battle.

Same-sex marriage advocates have primarily invoked *Loving* to argue, by analogy, that a ban on same-sex marriage is a form of sex discrimination, just as a ban on interracial marriage is a form of race discrimination. In *Loving*, Virginia argued its law was permissible because it barred whites from marrying non-whites, just as much as it barred non-whites from marrying whites. However, the Supreme Court expressly rejected this "equal application" justification, holding that the law was racially discriminatory because it determined eligibility to marry based on an individual's race.

The same logic, many have argued, applies to bans on same-sex marriage: a man is ineligible to marry another man solely because of his sex, and a woman ineligible to marry a woman because of her sex. And the fact that both sexes are equally forbidden from marrying same-sex partners does not negate this discrimination on the basis of sex.

The so-called *Loving* analogy was first made successfully in *Baehr v. Lewin*, a 1993 case in which the Hawaii Supreme Court set the stage for the legalization of same-sex marriage in that state. The court concluded that the ban on same-sex marriage constituted a sex-based classification, dooming it to almost certain invalidation at trial on remand, since such classifications are reviewed with strict scrutiny under the Hawaii Constitution. (In the end, same-sex marriage never became legal in Hawaii because of a subsequent amendment to the state's constitution.)

The court in *Baehr* also relied on *Loving* for another proposition: that state law cannot define marriage based on religious traditions. The trial court in *Loving* had justified Virginia's ban on interracial marriage because of the implicit endorsement of "Almighty God," who purportedly had separated the races by continent in order to keep them apart. By overturning the trial court's ruling, the Hawaii court wrote, the U.S. Supreme Court had rejected such religious influence on the definition of the right to marry. "[W]e do not believe," the Hawaii Supreme Court wrote, "that trial judges are the ultimate authorities on the subject of Divine Will, and, as *Loving* amply demonstrates, constitutional law may mandate, like it or not, that customs change with an evolving social order."

Later cases on same-sex marriage have also considered the import of *Loving*. The sex discrimination argument has been made in many cases, but with mixed results. Some courts have distinguished *Loving* from cases involving same-sex marriage primarily because of the courts' view that racial classifications are uniquely invidious and thus intolerable. In *Baker v. State*, for example, the Vermont Supreme Court interpreted the state constitution to require that equal benefits be extended to same-sex couples (codified ultimately in the nation's first civil union bill), but rejected the analogy to *Loving* as "flawed." As the court explained, "[w]e do not confront in this case the evil that was institutionalized racism"; moreover, plaintiffs "have not demonstrated that the exclusion of same-sex couples from the definition of marriage was intended to discriminate against women or lesbians and gay men, as racial segregation was designed to maintain the pernicious doctrine of white supremacy."

Other courts distinguished *Loving* by taking into account recent history and tradition to decide whether a fundamental right is at stake. In *Andersen v. Kings County*, a Washington state case, for example, the court observed that "whatever the history and tradition of interracial marriage had been, by the time *Loving* was decided, it had changed." In 1967, only 16 states still banned interracial marriage; in 2006, when *Andersen* was decided, only a single state permits same-sex marriage.

However, the only court to validate same-sex marriage interpreted *Loving* differently in this regard. The Massachusetts Supreme Judicial Court, in *Goodridge v. Department of Public Health*, concluded that *Loving's* outcome did not depend on the "full-scale retreat" of miscegenation laws, but turned instead on a "more fully developed understanding of the invidious quality of the discrimination."

Outside the same-sex marriage context, *Loving* has had little relevance, if any, in challenging state regulation of marriage. *Loving* is not cited at all in *Moe v. Dinkins*, a leading decision, issued by a judge of the U.S. District Court of the Southern District of New York in 1981, considering the constitutionality of a New York law providing that minors below a certain age can only marry with parental consent. Nor is it cited in *Utah v. Holm*, a very recent decision by the Utah Supreme Court upholding a man's conviction for bigamy against a constitutional challenge.

Loving v. Virginia in Other Legal Contexts

Loving was central to the development of constitutional protection for marriage, but also important to establishing a more fundamental principle: that state regulation of domestic relations is constrained by federal constitutional guarantees.

A decade before *Loving*, the validity of Virginia's anti-miscegenation law had been upheld, in *Naim v. Naim*, by the state's highest court on the grounds that "[m]arriage . . . is subject to the control of the States. Nearly seventy years ago the [U.S.] Supreme Court said, and it has said nothing to the contrary since." The U.S. Supreme Court refused to review this case, leaving that notion intact until it wrote in *Loving* that the power of the states to regulate marriage is not "unlimited" given the "commands of the Fourteenth Amendment."

This repudiation of unlimited state power over domestic relations had implications beyond the right to marry, and spurred an expansion of substantive due process rights to include a panoply of other rights. There is now a lengthy patchwork of cases cited for the proposition that individuals have "the right to be free, except in very limited circumstances, from unwanted governmental intrusions into one's privacy," and *Loving* is virtually always early in the list of citations.

Loving also had implications for cases having nothing to do with marriage or family. *Zablocki* made clear that *Loving* was not just a case about race, but other cases have made clear that it was also not just a case about marriage. Because of the centrality of race to the ruling in *Loving*, the opinion has had a robust life outside the family law context. Viewing the Virginia law as "designed to maintain White Supremacy," the Supreme Court in *Loving* took a hard line on racial classifications, not only rejecting the "equal application" theory the state had urged . . . but also applying the highest form of scrutiny to evaluate the law's constitutionality. Thus, *Loving* continues to be cited as one of the main precedents for the level of scrutiny applied to race-based classifications in a variety of contexts such as affirmative action, voting rights, and school financing.

Loving's Landmark Status Is Well-Deserved

Loving's landmark case status is, forty years later, firm and well-deserved. Its contribution to the canon of American law is unquestionable, as the precedent has shaped two important substantive constitutional doctrines and recalibrated the balance of federal-state power over domestic relations. These effects are an important part of the legacy of *Loving* that we celebrate today.

Though interracial marriage remains a disappointingly unusual occurrence, and the black-white cultural and marital divide is still deeply entrenched, *Loving* removed the legal obstacles to such relationships. That cultural change has lagged behind the legal change is no criticism of the Supreme Court's ruling in *Loving*, but simply a reflection of law's limited power to effect social change. Had *Loving* come out the other way, we would certainly not come together to celebrate its anniversaries.

Chapter 3

Refusing the Freedom to Die

Case Overview

Washington v. Glucksberg (1997)

Since becoming a U.S. territory in 1854, Washington, like most states, had outlawed suicide and prohibited anyone from assisting another in committing or attempting to commit "self-murder." The state's Natural Death Act, which was made law in 1979, stipulates that the withholding of life-sustaining equipment does not constitute suicide but also includes a clause specifically banning physician-assisted suicide. In 1994, the constitutionality of the Washington physician-assisted ban was challenged in court by Dr. Harold Glucksberg, along with four other medical doctors, three terminally ill patients (one dying of cancer, one dying of AIDS, and one dying of emphysema), and the nonprofit group Compassion in Dying. In their case in district court, the plaintiffs argued there is a liberty interest protected by the Fourteenth Amendment that extends to "a personal choice by a mentally competent terminally ill adult to commit physician-assisted suicide."

The district court ruled in favor of Glucksberg and the other plaintiffs, finding that terminally ill patients do indeed have a liberty interest protected by the Constitution to commit physician-assisted suicide, and that the Washington law was therefore unconstitutional. The state of Washington appealed to the U.S. Court of Appeals for the Ninth Circuit. They too agreed with the plaintiffs, finding that each person has a fundamental liberty interest in controlling the time and manner of their death, which is protected by the due process clause of the Fourteenth Amendment. The Washington statute banning assisted suicide was overturned. The state of Washington then took the high-profile case to the United States Supreme Court, which unanimously reversed the decisions of the district court and court of appeals.

In his opinion, Justice William Rehnquist reflected all nine justices' view that no fundamental right exists to assisted suicide. He said that in determining whether a liberty interest is "fundamental," and thus protected by the due process clause, the Court must first look to the nation's history to see if that liberty has been regarded as fundamental. He found that it clearly has not. Rehnquist also noted that the fundamental right must be carefully described and defined, which the Ninth Circuit Court failed to do properly—it referred to it variously as the "right to die," the "liberty to shape death" and the "right to control one's final days." The Supreme Court redefined the right as that of committing suicide with another's assistance and found that this is not a fundamental liberty interest protected by the due process clause. The Court also found that the Washington ban was rationally connected to many state interests, including prohibiting intentional killing and preserving human life; preventing the serious public health problem of suicide; maintaining physicians' roles as their patients' healers; and protecting the vulnerable from pressure to end their life.

The Court's decision made it clear that the Constitution does not protect a person's right to commit suicide and rejected the plaintiffs' request to overturn the Washington state ban on physician-assisted suicide. But while the ruling had the effect of upholding the laws of a majority of states that prohibit a person from assisting another in committing suicide, it left it up to each individual state to decide how to most appropriately deal with assisted suicide. As Rehnquist concluded in his opinion: "Throughout the Nation, Americans are engaged in an earnest and profound debate about the morality, legality, and practicality of physician-assisted suicide. Our holding permits this debate to continue, as it should in a democratic society." In 1997, Oregon legalized physician-assisted suicide, which has not been challenged in the state's courts.

> "The history of the law's treatment of
> assisted suicide in this country has been
> and continues to be one of the rejection
> of nearly all efforts to permit it."

The Court's Decision: The Government Can Regulate Some Liberties

William H. Rehnquist

William Hubbs Rehnquist was nominated by President Richard Nixon to the Supreme Court in 1971. After serving as associate justice for fifteen years, he was nominated in 1986 by President Ronald Reagan to be chief justice of the United States. Rehnquist's written opinion in the matter of Washington v. Glucksberg *reflects the unanimous agreement of the Court that the state could ban assisted suicide—although not all members of the Court agreed on the constitutionality of a total ban. In the case, Harold Glucksberg, a medical doctor, along with four other physicians, three terminal patients, and the organization Compassion in Dying, challenged the state of Washington's ban against assisted suicide. They argued that assisted suicide was a liberty interest protected by the due process clause of the Fourteenth Amendment. In his remarks, Rehnquist says that the due process clause does not prevent the government from regulating* all *conceivable liberties, only certain fundamental liberties that are "deeply rooted in the nation's history." He reviews Anglo-American law since the 1400s and shows that England and the colonies prohibited assisted suicides for centuries. The framers of*

William H. Rehnquist, *Washington, et al., Petitioners v. Harold Glucksberg et al.*, Supreme Court of the United States No. 96–110, 1997. Reproduced by permission.

the Constitution did not intend to break away from this tradition and establish a "right to die." Consequently, he says, it is not unconstitutional for a state to criminalize assisted suicide.

The question presented in this case is whether Washington's prohibition against "caus[ing]" or "aid[ing]" a suicide offends the Fourteenth Amendment to the United States Constitution. We hold that it does not. . . .

Our History and Practices

We begin, as we do in all due process cases, by examining our Nation's history, legal traditions, and practices. . . . In almost every State—indeed, in almost every western democracy—it is a crime to assist a suicide. The States' assisted-suicide bans are not innovations. Rather, they are longstanding expressions of the States' commitment to the protection and preservation of all human life. . . .

More specifically, for over 700 years, the Anglo-American common-law tradition has punished or otherwise disapproved of both suicide and assisting suicide. . . .

Assisted Suicide Reexamined

Though deeply rooted, the States' assisted-suicide bans have in recent years been reexamined and, generally, reaffirmed. Because of advances in medicine and technology, Americans today are increasingly likely to die in institutions, from chronic illnesses. Public concern and democratic action are therefore sharply focused on how best to protect dignity and independence at the end of life, with the result that there have been many significant changes in state laws and in the attitudes these laws reflect. Many States, for example, now permit "living wills," surrogate health-care decisionmaking, and the withdrawal or refusal of life-sustaining medical treatment. At the same time, however, voters and legislators continue for the most part to reaffirm their States' prohibitions on assisting suicide. . . .

Washington passed its Natural Death Act, which specifically stated that the "withholding or withdrawal of life-sustaining treatment . . . shall not, for any purpose, constitute a suicide" and that "[n]othing in this chapter shall be construed to condone, authorize, or approve mercy killing. . . ." In 1991, Washington voters rejected a ballot initiative which, had it passed, would have permitted a form of physician-assisted suicide. Washington then added a provision to the Natural Death Act expressly excluding physician-assisted suicide.

California voters rejected an assisted-suicide initiative similar to Washington's in 1993. On the other hand, in 1994, voters in Oregon enacted, also through ballot initiative, that State's "Death with Dignity Act," which legalized physician-assisted suicide for competent, terminally ill adults. Since the Oregon vote, many proposals to legalize assisted-suicide have been and continue to be introduced in the States' legislatures, but none has been enacted. And just last year [1996], Iowa and Rhode Island joined the overwhelming majority of States explicitly prohibiting assisted suicide. Also, on April 30, 1997, President Clinton signed the Federal Assisted Suicide Funding Restriction Act of 1997, which prohibits the use of federal funds in support of physician-assisted suicide.

Thus, the States are currently engaged in serious, thoughtful examinations of physician-assisted suicide and other similar issues. For example, New York State's Task Force on Life and the Law—an ongoing, blue-ribbon commission composed of doctors, ethicists, lawyers, religious leaders, and interested laymen—was convened in 1984 and commissioned with "a broad mandate to recommend public policy on issues raised by medical advances." Over the past decade, the Task Force has recommended laws relating to end-of-life decisions, surrogate pregnancy, and organ donation. After studying physician-assisted suicide, however, the Task Force unanimously concluded that "[l]egalizing assisted suicide and euthanasia would pose profound risks to many individuals who are ill and vulnerable. . . . [T]he potential dangers of this dramatic change in public policy would outweigh any benefit that might be achieved."

Attitudes toward suicide itself have changed . . . but our laws have consistently condemned, and continue to prohibit, assisting suicide. Despite changes in medical technology and notwithstanding an increased emphasis on the importance of end-of-life decisionmaking, we have not retreated from this prohibition. Against this backdrop of history, tradition, and practice, we now turn to respondents' constitutional claim.

The Protections of Due Process

The Due Process Clause guarantees more than fair process, and the "liberty" it protects includes more than the absence of physical restraint. . . . The Clause also provides heightened protection against government interference with certain fundamental rights and liberty interests. In a long line of cases, we have held that, in addition to the specific freedoms protected by the Bill of Rights, the "liberty" specially protected by the Due Process Clause includes the rights to marry, *Loving v. Virginia* (1967); to have children, *Skinner v. Oklahoma ex rel. Williamson* (1942); to direct the education and upbringing of one's children, *Meyer v. Nebraska* (1923); *Pierce v. Society of Sisters* (1925); to marital privacy, *Griswold v. Connecticut* (1965); to use contraception, *ibid.; Eisenstadt v. Baird* (1972); to bodily integrity, *Rochin v. California* (1952), and to abortion, *[Planned Parenthood v.] Casey* [(1992)], *supra.* We have also assumed, and strongly suggested, that the Due Process Clause protects the traditional right to refuse unwanted life-saving medical treatment.

But we "ha[ve] always been reluctant to expand the concept of substantive due process because guideposts for responsible decisionmaking in this unchartered area are scarce and open-ended." By extending constitutional protection to an asserted right or liberty interest, we, to a great extent, place the matter outside the arena of public debate and legislative action. We must therefore "exercise the utmost care whenever we are asked to break new ground in this field," lest the liberty protected by the Due Process Clause be subtly transformed into the policy preferences of the Members of this Court. . . .

Protection of the Asserted "Liberty" in This Case

The Washington statute at issue in this case prohibits "aid[ing] another person to attempt suicide," and, thus, the question before us is whether the "liberty" specially protected by the Due Process Clause includes a right to commit suicide which itself includes a right to assistance in doing so.

We now inquire whether this asserted right has any place in our Nation's traditions. Here, as discussed, we are confronted with a consistent and almost universal tradition that has long rejected the asserted right, and continues explicitly to reject it today, even for terminally ill, mentally competent adults. To hold for respondents, we would have to reverse centuries of legal doctrine and practice, and strike down the considered policy choice of almost every State.

Respondents contend, however, that the liberty interest they assert *is* consistent with this Court's substantive-due-process line of cases, if not with this Nation's history and practice. . . . The question presented in this case, however, is whether the protections of the Due Process Clause include a right to commit suicide with another's assistance. With this "careful description" of respondents' claim in mind, we turn to *Casey* and *Cruzan* [*v. Director, Missouri Department of Health*].

Cruzan and *Casey* as Precedents

Respondents contend that in *Cruzan* we "acknowledged that competent, dying persons have the right to direct the removal of life-sustaining medical treatment and thus hasten death," and that "the constitutional principle behind recognizing the patient's liberty to direct the withdrawal of artificial life support applies at least as strongly to the choice to hasten impending death by consuming lethal medication." Similarly, the Court of Appeals concluded that "*Cruzan*, by recognizing a liberty interest that includes the refusal of artificial provision of life-sustaining food and water, necessarily recognize[d] a liberty interest in hastening one's own death."

The right assumed in *Cruzan*, however, was not simply deduced from abstract concepts of personal autonomy. Given the common-law rule that forced medication was a battery, and the long legal tradition protecting the decision to refuse unwanted medical treatment, our assumption was entirely consistent with this Nation's history and constitutional traditions. The decision to commit suicide with the assistance of another may be just as personal and profound as the decision to refuse unwanted medical treatment, but it has never enjoyed similar legal protection. Indeed, the two acts are widely and reasonably regarded as quite distinct. In *Cruzan* itself, we recognized that most States outlawed assisted suicide—and even more do today—and we certainly gave no intimation that the right to refuse unwanted medical treatment could be somehow transmuted into a right to assistance in committing suicide. . . .

Respondents also rely on *Casey*. There, the Court's opinion concluded that "the essential holding of *Roe v. Wade* should be retained and once again reaffirmed." We held, first, that a woman has a right, before her fetus is viable, to an abortion "without undue interference from the State;" second, that States may restrict postviability abortions, so long as exceptions are made to protect a woman's life and health; and third, that the State has legitimate interests throughout a pregnancy in protecting the health of the woman and the life of the unborn child. In reaching this conclusion, the opinion discussed in some detail this Court's substantive-due-process tradition of interpreting the Due Process Clause to protect certain fundamental rights and "personal decisions relating to marriage, procreation, contraception, family relationships, child rearing, and education," and noted that many of those rights and liberties "involv[e] the most intimate and personal choices a person may make in a lifetime."

The Court of Appeals, like the District Court, found *Casey* "'highly instructive'" and "'almost prescriptive'" for determining "'what liberty interest may inhere in a terminally ill person's choice to commit suicide'":

> "Like the decision of whether or not to have an abortion, the decision how and when to die is one of 'the most intimate and personal choices a person may make in a lifetime,' a choice 'central to personal dignity and autonomy.'"

Similarly, respondents emphasize the statement in *Casey* that:

> "At the heart of liberty is the right to define one's own concept of existence, of meaning, of the universe, and of the mystery of human life. Beliefs about these matters could not define the attributes of personhood were they formed under compulsion of the State."

By choosing this language, the Court's opinion in *Casey* described, in a general way and in light of our prior cases, those personal activities and decisions that this Court has identified as so deeply rooted in our history and traditions, or so fundamental to our concept of constitutionally ordered liberty, that they are protected by the Fourteenth Amendment. The opinion moved from the recognition that liberty necessarily includes freedom of conscience and belief about ultimate considerations to the observation that "though the abortion decision may originate within the zone of conscience and belief, it is *more than a philosophic exercise.*" That many of the rights and liberties protected by the Due Process Clause sound in personal autonomy does not warrant the sweeping conclusion that any and all important, intimate, and personal decisions are so protected, and *Casey* did not suggest otherwise.

Suicide Is Not a Fundamental Liberty Interest

The history of the law's treatment of assisted suicide in this country has been and continues to be one of the rejection of nearly all efforts to permit it. That being the case, our decisions lead us to conclude that the asserted "right" to assistance in committing suicide is not a fundamental liberty interest protected by the Due Process Clause. The Constitution also requires, however, that Washington's assisted-suicide ban be rationally related to legitimate government interests. . . . Washington's assisted-suicide ban implicates a number of state interests.

First, Washington has an "unqualified interest in the preservation of human life." The State's prohibition on assisted suicide, like all homicide laws, both reflects and advances its commitment to this interest. ("[T]he interests in the sanctity of life that are represented by the criminal homicide laws are threatened by one who expresses a willingness to participate in taking the life of another"). This interest is symbolic and aspirational as well as practical. . . .

Suicide as a Public Health Concern

[A]ll admit that suicide is a serious public health problem, especially among persons in otherwise vulnerable groups. . . . The State has an interest in preventing suicide, and in studying, identifying, and treating its causes. . . .

Those who attempt suicide—terminally ill or not—often suffer from depression or other mental disorders. . . . Research indicates, however, that many people who request physician-assisted suicide withdraw that request if their depression and pain are treated. . . .

Protecting Medical Ethics

The State also has an interest in protecting the integrity and ethics of the medical profession. . . . The American Medical Association, like many other medical and physicians' groups, has concluded that "[p]hysician-assisted suicide is fundamentally incompatible with the physician's role as healer." . . . and physician-assisted suicide could, it is argued, undermine the trust that is essential to the doctor-patient relationship by blurring the time-honored line between healing and harming. . . .

Protecting the Vulnerable

Next, the State has an interest in protecting vulnerable groups—including the poor, the elderly, and disabled persons—from abuse, neglect, and mistakes. The Court of Appeals dismissed the State's concern that disadvantaged persons might be pressured into physician-assisted suicide as "ludicrous on its face." We have recognized, however, the real risk of subtle coercion and undue influence in end-of-life situations. Similarly, the New York Task Force warned that "[l]egalizing physician-assisted suicide would pose profound risks to many individuals who are ill and vulnerable. . . . The risk of harm is greatest for the many individuals in our society whose autonomy and well-being are already compromised by poverty, lack of access to good medical care, advanced age, or membership in a stigmatized social group." . . . If physician-assisted suicide were permitted, many might resort to it to spare their families the substantial financial burden of end-of-life health-care costs.

The State's interest here goes beyond protecting the vulnerable from coercion; it extends to protecting disabled and terminally ill people from prejudice, negative and inaccurate stereotypes, and "societal indifference." The State's assisted-suicide ban reflects and reinforces its policy that the lives of terminally ill, disabled, and elderly people must be no less valued than the lives of the young and healthy, and that a seriously disabled person's suicidal impulses should be interpreted and treated the same way as anyone else's. . . .

A Continuing Debate

We need not weigh exactingly the relative strengths of these various interests. They are unquestionably important and legitimate, and Washington's ban on assisted suicide is at least reasonably related to their promotion and protection. We therefore hold that Wash. Rev. Code § 9A.36.060(1) (1994) does not violate the Fourteenth Amendment, either on its face or "as applied to competent, terminally ill adults who wish to hasten their deaths by obtaining medication prescribed by their doctors."

Throughout the Nation, Americans are engaged in an earnest and profound debate about the morality, legality, and practicality of physician-assisted suicide. Our holding permits this debate to continue, as it should in a democratic society.

"[The] decision could only be justified by the momentous proposition ... that an American citizen does not, after all, have the rights ... to live and die in the light of his own religious and ethical beliefs ..."

Choosing Life or Death Is a Personal Matter

Ronald Dworkin, Thomas Nagel, Robert Nozick, John Rawls, T.M. Scanlon, and Judith Jarvis Thomson

Ronald Dworkin is Frank Henry Sommer Professor of Law and Philosophy at New York University and Jeremy Bentham Professor of Law and Philosophy at University College London. Thomas Nagel is university professor at New York University. Robert Nozick was a professor of moral philosophy at Harvard University. John Rawls was a professor of political philosophy at Harvard University. T.M. Scanlon is the Alford Professor of Natural Religion, Moral Philosophy, and Civil Polity in Harvard University's Department of Philosophy. Judith Jarvis Thomson is a professor emeritus at the Massachusetts Institute of Technology. In the following viewpoint taken from the "amicus brief" they submitted to the Supreme Court for the plaintiffs in Washington v. Glucksberg, *the six moral philosophers argue for a person's right to make decisions regarding life's value, and urge the Court to find for the plaintiffs. In the case, Dr. Harold Glucksberg, together with several physicians, patients, and the nonprofit organization Compassion in Dying, sought to challenge Washington*

Ronald Dworkin, Thomas Nagel, Robert Nozick, John Rawls, T.M. Scanlon, and Judith Jarvis Thomson, "Assisted Suicide: The Philosophers' Brief," *The New York Review of Books*, vol. 44, no. 5, March 27, 1997. Reprinted with permission from The New York Review of Books.

State's legal ban on physician-assisted suicide "as applied to competent, terminally ill adults who wish to hasten their deaths" by obtaining medication from their doctors. The philosophers point out that the liberty interests of the plaintiffs flow directly from previous Supreme Court decisions.

Amici ["friends"] are six moral and political philosophers who differ on many issues of public morality and policy. They are united, however, in their conviction that respect for fundamental principles of liberty and justice, as well as for the American constitutional tradition, requires that the decisions of the Courts of Appeals be affirmed.

Overview of the Argument

These cases do not invite or require the Court to make moral, ethical, or religious judgments about how people should approach or confront their death or about when it is ethically appropriate to hasten one's own death or to ask others for help in doing so. On the contrary, they ask the Court to recognize that individuals have a constitutionally protected interest in making those grave judgments for themselves, free from the imposition of any religious or philosophical orthodoxy by court or legislature. States have a constitutionally legitimate interest in protecting individuals from irrational, ill-informed, pressured, or unstable decisions to hasten their own death. To that end, states may regulate and limit the assistance that doctors may give individuals who express a wish to die. But states may not deny people in the position of the patient-plaintiffs in these cases the opportunity to demonstrate, through whatever reasonable procedures the state might institute—even procedures that err on the side of caution—that their decision to die is indeed informed, stable, and fully free. Denying that opportunity to terminally ill patients who are in agonizing pain or otherwise doomed to an existence they regard as intolerable could only be justified on the basis of a religious or ethical conviction about the value or meaning of life itself. Our Constitution forbids government to impose such convictions on its citizens.

Petitioners [i.e., the state authorities of Washington and New York] and the amici who support them offer two contradictory arguments. Some deny that the patient-plaintiffs have any constitutionally protected liberty interest in hastening their own deaths. But that liberty interest flows directly from this Court's previous decisions. It flows from the right of people to make their own decisions about matters "involving the most intimate and personal choices a person may make in a lifetime, choices central to personal dignity and autonomy" [*Planned Parenthood v. Casey* (1992)].

The Solicitor General, urging reversal in support of Petitioners, recognizes that the patient-plaintiffs do have a constitutional liberty interest at stake in these cases. . . .

The Solicitor General nevertheless argues that Washington and New York properly ignored this profound interest when they required the patient-plaintiffs to live on in circumstances they found intolerable. He argues that a state may simply declare that it is unable to devise a regulatory scheme that would adequately protect patients whose desire to die might be ill-informed or unstable or foolish or not fully free, and that a state may therefore fall back on a blanket prohibition. This Court has never accepted that patently dangerous rationale for denying protection altogether to a conceded fundamental constitutional interest. It would be a serious mistake to do so now. If that rationale were accepted, an interest acknowledged to be constitutionally protected would be rendered empty. . . .

The Liberty Interest Asserted Here Is Protected by the Due Process Clause

Certain decisions are momentous in their impact on the character of a person's life—decisions about religious faith, political and moral allegiance, marriage, procreation, and death, for example. Such deeply personal decisions pose controversial questions about how and why human life has value. In a free society, individuals must be allowed to make those decisions for themselves, out of their own faith, conscience, and convictions. This Court has insisted, in a variety of contexts and circumstances, that this great freedom is among those protected by the Due Process Clause as essential to a community of "ordered liberty." In its recent decision in *Planned Parenthood v. Casey*, the Court offered a paradigmatic statement of that principle:

> matters involving the most intimate and personal choices a person may make in a lifetime, choices central to a person's dignity and autonomy, are central to the liberty protected by the Fourteenth Amendment.

That declaration reflects an idea underlying many of our basic constitutional protections. As the Court explained in *West Virginia State Board of Education v. Barnette* (1943):

> If there is any fixed star in our constitutional constellation, it is that no official . . . can prescribe what shall be orthodox in politics, nationalism, religion, or other matters of opinion or force citizens to confess by word or act their faith therein.

A person's interest in following his own convictions at the end of life is so central a part of the more general right to make "intimate and personal choices" for himself that a failure to protect that particular interest would undermine the general right altogether. Death is, for each of us, among the most significant events of life. As the Chief Justice said in *Cruzan v. Missouri* (1999) "[t]he choice between life and death is a deeply personal decision of obvious and overwhelming finality." Most of us see death—whatever we think will follow it—as the final act of life's drama, and we want that last act to reflect our own convictions, those we have tried to live by, not the convictions of others forced on us in our most vulnerable moment.

Different people, of different religious and ethical beliefs, embrace very different convictions about which way of dying confirms and which contradicts the value of their lives. Some fight against death with every weapon their doctors can devise. Others will do nothing to hasten death even if they pray it will come soon. Still others, including the patient-plaintiffs in these cases, want to end their lives when they think that living on, in the only way they can, would disfigure rather than enhance the lives they had created. Some people make the latter choice not just to escape pain. Even if it were possible to eliminate all pain for a dying patient—and frequently that is not possible—that would not end or even much alleviate the anguish some would feel at remaining alive, but intubated, helpless, and often sedated near oblivion.

None of these dramatically different attitudes about the meaning of death can be dismissed as irrational. None should be imposed, either by the pressure of doctors or relatives or by the fiat of government, on people who reject it. Just as it would be intolerable for government to dictate that doctors never be permitted to try to keep someone alive as long as possible, when that is what the patient wishes, so it is intolerable for government to dictate that doctors may never, under any circumstances, help someone to die who believes that further life means only degradation. The Constitution insists that people must be free to make these deeply personal decisions for themselves and must not be forced to end their lives in a way that appalls them, just because that is what some majority thinks proper.

Casey Supports the Liberty Interest Asserted Here

In *Casey*, this Court, in holding that a state cannot constitutionally proscribe abortion in all cases, reiterated that the Constitution protects a sphere of autonomy in which individuals must be permitted to make certain decisions for themselves. The Court began its analysis by pointing out that "[a]t the heart of liberty is the right to define one's own concept of existence, of meaning, of the universe, and of the mystery of human life." Choices flowing out of these conceptions, on matters "involving the most intimate and personal choices a person may make in a lifetime, choices central to personal dignity and autonomy, are central to the liberty protected by the Fourteenth Amendment." "Beliefs about these matters," the Court continued, "could not define the attributes of person-hood were they formed under compulsion of the State."

In language pertinent to the liberty interest asserted here, the Court explained why decisions about abortion fall within this category of "personal and intimate" decisions. A decision whether or not to have an abortion, "originat[ing] within the zone of conscience and belief," involves conduct in which "the liberty of the woman is at stake in a sense unique to the human condition and so unique to the law." As such, the decision necessarily involves the very "destiny of the woman" and is inevitably "shaped to a large extent on her own conception of her spiritual imperatives and her place in society." Precisely because of these characteristics of the decision, "the State is [not] entitled to proscribe [abortion] in all instances." Rather, to allow a total prohibition on abortion would be to permit a state to impose one conception of the meaning and value of human existence on all individuals. This the Constitution forbids.

The Solicitor General nevertheless argues that the right to abortion could be supported on grounds other than this autonomy principle, grounds that would not apply here. He argues, for example, that the abortion right might flow from the great burden an unwanted child imposes on its mother's life. But whether or not abortion rights could be defended on such grounds, they were not the grounds on which this Court in fact relied. To the contrary, the Court explained at length that the right flows from the constitutional protection accorded all individuals to "define one's own concept of existence, of meaning, of the universe, and of the mystery of human life." The analysis in *Casey* compels the conclusion that the patient-plaintiffs have a liberty interest in this case that a state cannot burden with a blanket prohibition. Like a woman's decision whether to have an abortion, a decision to die involves one's very "destiny" and inevitably will be "shaped to a large extent on [one's] own conception of [one's] spiritual imperatives and [one's] place in society." Just as a blanket prohibition on abortion would involve the improper imposition of one conception of the meaning and value of human existence on all individuals, so too would a blanket prohibition on assisted suicide. The liberty interest asserted here cannot be rejected without undermining the rationale of *Casey*. Indeed, the lower court opinions in the Washington case expressly recognized the parallel between the liberty interest in *Casey* and the interest asserted here. . . . This Court should do the same.

Cruzan Supports the Liberty Interest Asserted Here

We agree with the Solicitor General that this Court's decision in "*Cruzan* . . . supports the conclusion that a liberty interest is at stake in this case." Petitioners, however, insist that the present cases can be distinguished because the right at issue in *Cruzan* was limited to a right to reject an unwanted invasion of one's body. But this Court repeatedly has held that in appropriate circumstances a state may require individuals to accept unwanted invasions of the body. . . .

The liberty interest at stake in *Cruzan* was a more profound one. If a competent patient has a constitutional right to refuse life-sustaining treatment, then, the Court implied, the state could not override that right. The regulations upheld in *Cruzan* were designed only to ensure that the individual's wishes were ascertained correctly. Thus, if *Cruzan* implies a right of competent patients to refuse life-sustaining treatment, that implication must be understood as resting not simply on a right to refuse bodily invasions but on the more profound right to refuse medical intervention when what is at stake is a momentous personal decision, such as the timing and manner of one's death. In her concurrence, Justice [Sandra Day] O'Connor expressly recognized that the right at issue involved a "deeply personal decision" that is "inextricably intertwined" with our notion of "self-determination."

Cruzan also supports the proposition that a state may not burden a terminally ill patient's liberty interest in determining the time and manner of his death by prohibiting doctors from terminating life support. Seeking to distinguish *Cruzan*, Petitioners insist that a state may nevertheless burden that right in a different way by forbidding doctors to assist in the suicide of patients who are not on life-support machinery. They argue that doctors who remove life support are only allowing a natural process to end in death whereas doctors who prescribe lethal drugs are intervening to cause death. So, according to this argument, a state has an independent justification for forbidding doctors to assist in suicide that it does not have for forbidding them to remove life support. In the former case though not the latter, it is said, the state forbids an act of killing that is morally much more problematic than merely letting a patient die.

This argument is based on a misunderstanding of the pertinent moral principles. It is certainly true that when a patient does not wish to die, different acts, each of which foreseeably results in his death, nevertheless have very different moral status. When several patients need organ transplants and organs are scarce, for example, it is morally permissible for a doctor to deny an organ to one patient, even though he will die without it, in order to give it to another. But it is certainly not permissible for a doctor to kill one patient in order to use his organs to save another. The morally significant difference between those two acts is not, however, that killing is a positive act and not providing an organ is a mere omission, or that killing someone is worse than merely allowing a "natural" process to result in death. It would be equally impermissible for a doctor to let an injured patient bleed to death, or to refuse antibiotics to a patient with pneumonia—in each case the doctor would have allowed death to result from a "natural" process—in order to make his organs available for transplant to others. A doctor violates his patient's rights whether the doctor acts or refrains from acting, against the patient's wishes, in a way that is designed to cause death.

When a competent patient does want to die, the moral situation is obviously different, because then it makes no sense to appeal to the patient's right not to be killed as a reason why an act designed to cause his death is impermissible. From the patient's point of view, there is no morally pertinent difference between a doctor's terminating treatment that keeps him alive, if that is what he wishes, and a doctor's helping him to end his own life by providing lethal pills he may take himself, when ready, if that is what he wishes—except that the latter may be quicker and more humane. Nor is that a pertinent difference from the doctor's point of view. If and when it is permissible for him to act with death in view, it does not matter which of those two means he and his patient choose. If it is permissible for a doctor deliberately to withdraw medical treatment in order to allow death to result from a natural process, then it is equally permissible for him to help his patient hasten his own death more actively, if that is the patient's express wish. . . .

State Interests Do Not Justify a Categorical Prohibition on All Assisted Suicide

Of course, a state has important interests that justify regulating physician-assisted suicide. It may be legitimate for a state to deny an opportunity for assisted suicide when it acts in what it reasonably judges to be the best interests of the potential suicide, and when its judgment on that issue does not rest on contested judgments about "matters involving the most intimate and personal choices a person may make in a lifetime, choices central to personal dignity and autonomy." A state might assert, for example, that people who are not terminally ill, but who have formed a desire to die, are, as a group, very likely later to be grateful if they are prevented from taking their own lives. It might then claim that it is legitimate, out of concern for such people, to deny any of them a doctor's assistance [in taking their own lives].

This Court need not decide now the extent to which such paternalistic interests might override an individual's liberty interest. No one can plausibly claim, however—and it is noteworthy that neither Petitioners nor the Solicitor General does claim—that any such prohibition could serve the interests of any significant number of terminally ill patients. On the contrary, any paternalistic justification for an absolute prohibition of assistance to such patients would of necessity appeal to a widely contested religious or ethical conviction many of them, including the patient-plaintiffs, reject. Allowing *that* justification to prevail would vitiate the liberty interest.

Even in the case of terminally ill patients, a state has a right to take all reasonable measures to insure that a patient requesting such assistance has made an informed, competent, stable and uncoerced decision. It is plainly legitimate for a state to establish procedures through which professional and administrative judgments can be made about these matters, and to forbid doctors to assist in suicide when its reasonable procedures have not been satisfied. States may be permitted considerable leeway in designing such procedures. They may be permitted, within reason, to err on what they take to be the side of caution. But they may not use the bare possibility of error as justification for refusing to establish any procedures at all and relying instead on a flat prohibition.

Choosing Death While Mentally Competent

Each individual has a right to make the "most intimate and personal choices central to personal dignity and autonomy." That right encompasses the right to exercise some control over the time and manner of one's death.

The patient-plaintiffs in these cases were all mentally competent individuals in the final phase of terminal illness and died within months of filing their claims.

Jane Doe described how her advanced cancer made even the most basic bodily functions such as swallowing, coughing, and yawning extremely painful and that it was "not possible for [her] to reduce [her] pain to an acceptable level of comfort and to retain an alert state." Faced with such circumstances, she sought to be able to "discuss freely with [her] treating physician [her] intention of hastening [her] death through the consumption of drugs prescribed for that purpose."

George A. Kingsley, in advanced stages of AIDS which included, among other hardships, the attachment of a tube to an artery in his chest which made even routine functions burdensome and the development of lesions on his brain, sought advice from his doctors regarding prescriptions which could hasten his impending death.

Jane Roe, suffering from cancer since 1988, had been almost completely bedridden since 1993 and experienced constant pain which could not be alleviated by medication. After undergoing counseling for herself and her family, she desired to hasten her death by taking prescription drugs.

John Doe, who had experienced numerous AIDS-related ailments since 1991, was "especially cognizant of the suffering imposed by a lingering terminal illness because he was the primary caregiver for his long-term companion who died of AIDS" and sought prescription drugs from his physician to hasten his own death after entering the terminal phase of AIDS.

137

James Poe suffered from emphysema which caused him "a constant sensation of suffocating" as well as a cardiac condition which caused severe leg pain. Connected to an oxygen tank at all times but unable to calm the panic reaction associated with his feeling of suffocation even with regular doses of morphine, Mr. Poe sought physician-assisted suicide.

Rational Decisions Must Be Honored

A state may not deny the liberty claimed by the patient-plaintiffs in these cases without providing them an opportunity to demonstrate, in whatever way the state might reasonably think wise and necessary, that the conviction they expressed for an early death is competent, rational, informed, stable, and uncoerced.

Affirming the decisions by the Courts of Appeals would establish nothing more than that there is such a constitutionally protected right in principle. It would establish only that some individuals, whose decisions for suicide plainly cannot be dismissed as irrational or foolish or premature, must be accorded a reasonable opportunity to show that their decision for death is informed and free. It is not necessary to decide precisely which patients are entitled to that opportunity. If, on the other hand, this Court reverses the decisions below, its decision could only be justified by the momentous proposition—a proposition flatly in conflict with the spirit and letter of the Court's past decisions—that an American citizen does not, after all, have the right, even in principle, to live and die in the light of his own religious and ethical beliefs, his own convictions about why his life is valuable and where its value lies.

"[Gluckberg's] assumption that physician-assisted suicide can be confined to a mentally competent person in the final stage of a terminal illness who voluntarily wishes to end his or her life is naive."

Liberty and Personal Autonomy Are Not the Same

Edward Mcglynn Gaffney

Edward McGlynn Gaffney is a professor of law at Valparaiso University School of Law. In the following viewpoint, he discusses the merits and shortcomings of the plaintiffs' case in Washington v. Glucksberg. *Dr. Harold Glucksberg, four other doctors, three patients, and the organization Compassion in Dying argued in the case that the Washington state ban on physician-assisted suicide violated the due process clause. Gaffney argues against this view, stating that while liberty and equality are noble values, they should not diminish respect for human life. He notes too that the Fourteenth Amendment, to which the plaintiffs are looking for support for their case, states that people cannot be deprived of their "life, liberty, or property without due process of law," which implies that life and liberty are not to be considered mutually exclusive. Gaffney also takes issue with the idea, which he believes is at the heart of the* Glucksberg *defense, that liberty and personal autonomy are the same. He also counters the notion that there is a clear correlation between physician-assisted suicide and freedom, and provides several examples from history to demonstrate his point.*

Edward McGlynn Gaffney, "Liberty Interests," *Commonweal*, vol. 124, no. 9, May 9, 1997. Copyright 1997 Commonweal Foundation. Reproduced by permission of Commonweal Foundation.

Until Oregon amended its constitution in 1994, all fifty states prohibited physician-assisted suicide, either expressly or implicitly but unambiguously in the criminal sanctions for homicide. Two of the most publicized cases before the Supreme Court this year—*Washington v. Glucksberg* and *Vacco v. Quill*—could require all the states to abandon these laws. *Glucksberg* asks whether the due process clause of the Fourteenth Amendment protects the liberty of patients to end their own lives by seeking the assistance of a doctor, and whether doctors are free to provide this "service" to their patients. *Quill* questions whether a state violates the equal protection clause of the Fourteenth Amendment if it draws a line between letting a patient die and actively causing a patient's death.

Liberty and equality are noble values in our constitutional order, but neither liberty nor equality should diminish our respect for human life. The very text of the Fourteenth Amendment relied upon by those promoting physician-assisted suicide poses a serious difficulty: "No state can deprive any person of *life*, liberty, or property without due process or law . . . nor shall [it] deprive any person of equal protection of the laws" (emphasis added). The framers of this provision clearly thought of life, liberty, and equality as harmonious goals, not as mutual contradictions. It is a stretch to think of terminating life as a constitutional means of promoting liberty or equality.

Liberty and Self-Autonomy Are Not Synonymous

The principal argument in *Glucksberg* is that the human person should be free to decide not only when but how to die. This argument equates liberty with personal autonomy, exalting the freely choosing self. It acknowledges the possibility of abuse if physician-assisted suicide were to be normalized, but the only boundaries with which it concerns itself are those that protect the voluntary character of suicide. Its assumption that physician-assisted suicide can be confined to a mentally competent person in the final stages of a terminal illness who voluntarily wishes to end his or her life is naive. Each of the key terms—terminal illness, competence, and voluntariness—is an ambivalent, empty vessel waiting to be filled with the ideology of those who wish to embark on a grand social experiment on the issues of life and death.

But the fundamental flaw is the argument's misconception of constitutional liberty. It is true that some liberties should not depend on the outcome of elections. Earlier this century the Court began to give special protection to religious freedom, freedom of speech, and of the press, calling them "fundamental liberties" because it would be hard to conceive of our society without them. When the political branches enact laws that abridge these basic civil liberties, we should rejoice that a vigilant Court would nullify these laws as violations of the Constitution. But since the customs and traditions of our people have never thought of taking one's own life—let alone of assisting another to do so—as a fundamental liberty, the judiciary should defer to the political process on this issue. Several justices reminded counsel at oral argument that the states are entitled to considerable judicial deference in choosing among policy alternatives.

No Clear Correlation Between Assisted Suicide and Freedom

The argument in *Glucksberg* assumes rather than demonstrates a correlation between physician-assisted suicide and human freedom. The empirical evidence of this century in two dramatically different instances—Germany in the Nazi period and the Netherlands in the past decade—suggests that the outcome of doctors helping people to die is utter disregard for human freedom and human dignity. In the Nazi eugenics project, Hitler's doctors, not autonomous choosing patients, decided who was "worthy of life." In modern Holland, hundreds of doctors have admitted that they, not their patients, have decided the "right" moment for the patient to die.

Add to these historical episodes the phenomenon of "managed care" currently sweeping through medical practice in our country. Under these circumstances the motive for recommending the "quick way out" may not be compassion—a virtue that means identifying and even suffering with a patient—but simply raw economic self-interest.

In *Vacco v. Quill*, the argument is that it is irrational for New York to allow doctors to provide a variety of pain-killers but to prohibit the prescription of a lethal dose to a dying patient. But as with the liberty argument in *Glucksberg*, the argument in *Quill* misconceives the meaning of constitutional equality. The Constitution mandates that judges strike down laws that assault the equal dignity of persons before the law, but it does not give judges a roving warrant to invalidate all legislation which they find offensive or unwise. The most notorious examples of laws held to violate the equal protection clause were the Jim Crow laws. When the Court began to repudiate these laws in *Brown v. Board of Education* (1954), it was acting consistently with the purpose and meaning of the Fourteenth Amendment. And when, more recently, it began to invalidate laws that, in Justice William Brennan's phrase, placed women "more in a cage than on a pedestal," it was once again promoting the equal dignity of all persons before the law, irrespective of gender. But the laws prohibiting physician-assisted suicide are not based on hostility to anyone because of race or gender. On the contrary, these laws promote the equal value of the lives of all persons.

Glucksberg Will Not Promote Equal Justice

If it is by no means clear in *Glucksberg* that physician-assisted suicide would insure human freedom, it is even more dubious in *Quill* that physician-assisted suicide would promote equal justice. The probability is high that it would impose far more serious burdens on the poor, minorities, and the disabled. As Judge John T. Noonan, Jr., noted in his opinion in the Ninth Circuit, these groups "would be especially open to manipulation." For example, wrote Noonan, "when the nondisabled say they want to die, they are labeled as suicidal; if they are disabled, it is treated as 'natural' or 'reasonable'. . . . An insidious bias against the handicapped—again coupled with a cost-saving mentality—makes them especially in need of statutory protection."

On the day the Court heard argument in these cases, hundreds of disabled protesters in wheelchairs reinforced Noonan's point, chanting outside the Court, "We're not dead yet." Whether the Court heard this chant in so many words, it should be careful about the enormous implications for our culture that flow from thinking of physician-assisted suicide as a constitutional right grounded in either liberty or equality.

> "Although abortion precedents were in-
> voked less than a handful of times dur-
> ing the two hours, they clearly were
> never far from the justices' minds."

Abortion Is the Subtext in *Glucksberg*

Marcia Coyle

Marcia Coyle is a staff reporter for the National Law Journal. *In the following viewpoint, she discusses the liberty interest in Washington v. Glucksberg. In this case, five physicians, three patients, and a nonprofit organization sought to overturn a Washington State ban on physician-assisted suicide. Coyle re- ports that Laurence Tribe, who represented several New York pa- tients, explained to the Court that the liberty interest protected in the Constitution was that of the terminally ill, mentally com- petent individual, who when faced with imminent death, would not have to endure agonizing pain and suffering that can be re- lieved only by drug-induced unconsciousness. Tribe, along with Kathryn Tucker, the counsel for the Washington patients, stated that there is a constellation of interests flowing from personal autonomy and human dignity, all of which are within the sphere of liberty protected by the Fourteenth Amendment. Coyle ex- plains as well that during the trial, abortion precedents and es- pecially* Planned Parenthood v. Casey *(1992) were not far from the justices' minds; assisted suicide was the focus, but abortion was the subtext. But the question in the end was whether* Casey's *reach could legitimately extend to this case.*

Marcia Coyle, "What's Liberty's Scope?" *National Law Journal*, vol. 19, no. 21, January 1997, pp. A1, A18. Reproduced by permission.

W ith less than a minute remaining in back-to-back, two-hour-long arguments on the constitutionality of physician-assisted suicide, U.S. Supreme Court Justice John Paul Stevens leaned forward and asked Harvard Law School's Laurence H. Tribe the $64,000 question: "What is the liberty interest?"

It was a question Professor Tribe clearly had been hoping to address from the beginning of his 30-minute appearance but never had the chance to because of the justices' fast-paced questioning on other issues. And the question was one to which Professor Tribe, even though he was defending an appellate decision based on equal protection principles, had devoted most of his merits brief.

It was also the question that had to be answered first in these challenges, not last, Justice Anthony M. Kennedy had noted nearly two hours before Justice Stevens spoke, explaining, "The analysis is usually to determine whether there is a liberty interest at the outset."

The Liberty Interests—Not to Be Forced to Endure Suffering

The liberty interest protected by the Constitution. Professor Tribe told Justice Stevens, is the interest of the terminally ill, mentally competent individual, "when facing imminent death," not to be forced by the government to endure agonizing pain and suffering that can be relieved only by drug-induced unconsciousness.

This liberty interest, he and co-counsel, Kathryn Tucker, of Seattle's Perkins Coie, contend, implicates a "constellation of interests" flowing from personal autonomy and human dignity, all of which are within the substantive sphere of liberty protected by the 14th Amendment.

"Lovely philosophy," said Justice Antonin Scalia. "All of this is in the Constitution?" "*Casey* said as much," Professor Tribe answered, referring to the high court's most recent abortion ruling, *Planned Parenthood v. Casey*, (1992). Unless *Casey* is isolated to the abortion context, he and others believe, the high court must recognize the protected liberty interest of this category of patients who want and need a physician's assistance in carrying out this most personal decision.

Abortion Loomed Large

Casey and the high court's experience with post-*Roe v. Wade* abortion litigation loomed in the background of the intense and complex arguments Jan. 8 in *Vacco v. Quill*, and *Washington v. Glucksberg*, the two cases in which Professor Tribe and Ms. Tucker defended, and New York and Washington challenged, circuit court rulings that struck down the two states' bans on assisted suicide.

Although abortion precedents were invoked less than a handful of times during the two hours, they clearly were never far from the justices' minds.

For example, when Ms. Tucker told the court she was asking it to protect the terminally ill patient's choice but not to legislate its regulation, Chief Justice William H. Rehnquist predicted that ultimately, "You're going to have the same things as in abortion. How far do we go in regulating this? It will be a constitutional case in each one." And Justice Sandra Day O'Connor added, "I have no doubt it would result in a flow of cases for heaven knows how long."

By the end of the arguments, it appeared that many justices were reluctant to overturn the laws in 49 states. What was less clear was whether they would, in the words of Professor Tribe, isolate *Casey*, heavily relied on by the 9th U.S. Circuit Court of Appeals in *Glucksberg*.

"Like the decision of whether or not to have an abortion, the decision how and when to die is one of 'the most intimate and personal choices a person may make in a lifetime,' a choice 'central to personal dignity and autonomy,'" the appellate court said, quoting *Casey*.

Planned Parenthood v. Casey as Precendent

In the privacy of their conference room and chambers, the justices face the question of whether a liberty interest exists here, made perhaps more complicated by the urging of some staunch *Casey* proponents to isolate the decision, say some constitutional scholars.

Supporting the state bans on assisted suicide, the solicitor general of the United States nevertheless argued that a competent, terminally ill adult does have a liberty interest in obtaining relief from severe pain or suffering. But that interest cannot be equated with the interest recognized in *Casey*, he contended.

Although relief from pain and suffering is also part of the interest underlying the right to choose an abortion, he argued, that right implicates much more than the interest at stake in the assisted-suicide context. It implicates the ability of women to participate equally in the nation's economic and social life. He urged the justices to look to another line of precedents and its last right-to-die case, *Cruzan v. Director, Missouri Department of Health* (1990), to find the liberty interest he defined.

But ultimately, the solicitor general concluded, "overriding state interests," such as preventing abuse, justify state assisted-suicide bans.

On the opposite side, the New York-based Center for Reproductive Law & Policy—whose vice president, Kathryn Kolbert, argued and won the reaffirmation of the right to abortion in *Casey*—agrees with the solicitor general's characterization of the abortion right as unique and stresses the "important differences" between the two liberty interests.

The justices don't even have to consider its abortion precedents to decide the Washington case, Ms. Kolbert insists. By relying on other bodily integrity and personal autonomy precedents, primarily *Cruzan*, the court will find that a terminally ill person has a protected liberty interest in seeking medication to hasten death.

Both the Clinton administration and pro-abortion rights advocates have a common interest in ensuring no erosion of *Casey*, says constitutional law scholar Douglas Kmiec, of Notre Dame Law School.

"The solicitor general sought to convince the court it could decide these cases by declining to find a right to assisted suicide and in so declining, it would not jeopardize the abortion precedent," he says. "In order to do those mental gymnastics, the solicitor general had to re-center the *Roe* and *Casey* analysis from liberty to equality. But that is not the rationale the court has used."

Casey says that at the heart of liberty is the right to define one's own existence or place in the universe. Professor Kmiec explains, adding, "If that's the operating principle, it's very hard to distinguish the abortion cases from assisted-suicide cases."

Protecting *Casey*

Abortion supporters may feel Justice Kennedy might be in "an uncomfortable position if he had to take *Roe* at its core and say there is a right to personal autonomy that says I can do what I want with my body," adds Supreme Court and abortion scholar Associate Dean Christine Kellett, of Dickinson School of Law.

"I think they want to hold onto Kennedy, [Justice David H.] Souter and O'Connor—who wrote *Casey*—in future cases," she says. "While the court hasn't taken an abortion test lately, some states are now pushing a raft of laws testing the envelope of *Casey*, and the court is bound to see it again."

But Ms. Kolbert says she has no fear *Casey* will be eroded if linked to the assisted suicide cause: "Frankly, the effort to rely on *Casey* shows its central position within the jurisprudence of privacy, and that's a very good development."

Since the decision in 1992, *Casey* has stood, outside of the abortion context, not so much for substantive due process and privacy as for its discussion of stare decisis, say some scholars.

But *Casey* has appeared in some cases involving implied constitutional rights, says Professor Kmiec, most recently in parental rights litigation. He and others believe it will figure in future cases involving gay rights and school finance.

Besides the assisted suicide challenges, the high court may have something more to say about *Casey's* reach when it decides a case argued the day before those challenges—*U.S. v. Lanier.* Dissenting 6th Circuit judges relied on the abortion precedent to dispute the majority's holding that the Supreme Court has never specifically held there is a federal constitutional right to be free from interference with bodily integrity and so freedom from sexual assault cannot be a part of the right.

> "As was the case with abortion before
> Roe v. Wade . . . whether or not you
> have the right to die through assisted
> suicide will . . . depend on where you
> live."

States Can Decide if There Is a Right to Die

Michael G. Trachtman

*Michael G. Trachtman, a Pennsylvania attorney, was named
2007 winner of the Pennsylvania Bar's "Plain English" Committee Clarity Award for his efforts at conveying legal principles to
the public in understandable language. He provides a straightforward analysis in this viewpoint of* Washington v. Glucksberg,
*in which a group of doctors, patients, and a right-to-die group
sought to overturn Washington State's ban on physician-assisted
suicide. Trachtman notes that the litigants based their case on
the due process clause of the Fourteenth Amendment and explains the Court's decision. Trachtman ends by noting that although the Washington State ban was not overturned by the Supreme Court, the ruling permitted states to allow or prohibit
assisted suicides if they choose, as Oregon has done.*

Suppose a close friend becomes terminally ill, all quality of
life has evaporated, and he is suffering. Moreover, his medical bills will dissipate his assets, and he is desperately worried
about his family's financial future. He tells you he would prefer to die—peacefully, without pain, now. He pleads with you,

Michael G. Trachtman, "*Washington v. Glucksberg*," *The Supremes' Greatest Hits: The 34
Supreme Court Cases That Most Directly Affect Your Life.* New York: Sterling Publishing
Company, Inc., 2007. © 2007 by Sterling Publishing. All rights reserved. Reproduced by
permission.

as his closest friend, to help him carry out his wishes. All you need to do is fill an old painkiller prescription he has, give him the bottle, and he will do the rest. May you do it? May you arrange for a doctor or nurse to help him, and even if you could, would they be permitted to do anything?

As of this writing, forty-nine states prohibit assisted suicide, and in recent years doctors, terminally ill patients, and "death with dignity" organizations have challenged the constitutionality of these laws in court. One such challenge was mounted in the mid-1990s by Dr. Harold Glucksberg, along with other physicians, patients, and a nonprofit advocacy group. It involved a Washington State statute that makes "promoting a suicide" a felony. Glucksberg sought the right to honor the wishes of terminal patients who asked for his assistance. The case, *Washington v. Glucksberg*, made its way to the Supreme Court in 1997.

The Limits of Liberty

Glucksberg, like most litigants who have challenged assisted suicide bans, based his case on the historic Due Process Clause of the Fourteenth Amendment, which prohibits a state from depriving persons of "life, liberty, or property without due process of law." Surely, Glucksberg contended, this constitutional right of liberty must include the right of a competent adult to choose to die, and to seek assistance in implementing that decision. As the saying goes, it's a free country.

Some lower courts had agreed with this argument in other cases, but the Supreme Court, in an opinion written by Chief Justice [William] Rehnquist, unanimously disagreed. The Court found that the Due Process Clause does not prevent government from regulating all conceivable liberties, but only certain *fundamental* liberties rooted in the nation's history and traditions. The Court reviewed Anglo-American law since the 1400s, and found that England, and then the colonies, had prohibited assisted suicides for hundreds of years. Therefore, the Court ruled, there was no reason to believe that the framers of the Constitution intended to contravene this tradition and establish a "right to die." Consequently, said the Court, it was not unconstitutional for a state to criminalize assisted suicide.

States Can Allow or Ban Assisted Suicide

Keep in mind, however, that while *Washington v. Glucksberg* stands for the proposition that states may lawfully prohibit assisted suicides within their borders, states may also allow assisted suicides if they wish. So far, Oregon is the only state to have done so, enacting the Death with Dignity Act, which became effective in 1997. The law permits physicians, in well-defined circumstances, to provide a lethal dosage of pills to terminally ill patients who seek to end their own suffering. It is then up to the patient to take the pills, or not. The Bush administration challenged the constitutionality of the Death with Dignity Act and, in January 2006, the Supreme Court, while not endorsing the law, refused to overturn it, in a 6-3 vote. Several other states were awaiting the outcome of this ruling, and will now likely introduce similar legislation.

As was the case with abortion before *Roe v. Wade* (and as will be the case if *Roe* is overruled), whether or not you have the right to die through assisted suicide will, for the foreseeable future, depend on where you live.

CHAPTER 4

Allowing Sexual Liberty Between Consenting Adults

Case Overview

Lawrence and Garner v. Texas (2003)

Shortly before 10:30 p.m. on September 17, 1998, an unidenti-
fied man called the Harris County, Texas, Sheriff's Department and told the dispatcher that "a black male, armed with a
gun" was "going crazy" in the apartment next door. Two deputies responded to the call, entering the apartment of John
Lawrence to investigate the disturbance. The deputies discovered no intruder or weapon, but claimed they saw Lawrence
and another man, Tyron Garner, engaging in anal sex. The
two men were arrested and spent the night in jail. They
pleaded no contest to the charges and were convicted for sodomy under Texas's Homosexual Conduct law. They were fined
$200 and considered sex offenders in several states.

The caller was revealed to be Robert Eubanks, Garner's ro-
mantic partner, who was jealous that his lover was next door
with their mutual friend; he was eventually charged with making a false report. Lawrence and Garner, on the advice on lawyers from the Lambda Legal Defense and Education Fund,
which defends gay men and lesbians, appealed to the Texas
Court of Appeals and Criminal Court of Appeals, arguing that
the Texas statute under which they were convicted violated the
due process and equal protection clauses of the Fourteenth
Amendment. The Lambda lawyers filed on right to privacy, or
substantive due process, grounds claiming the State had no
right to punish consensual adult sex in a private residence.
And they maintained that the law violated their right to equal
protection because the Texas sodomy statue forbade certain
sexual behaviors between homosexuals but not heterosexual
couples. The Texas state courts upheld the convictions, relying
on the Supreme Court's 1986 ruling in *Bowers v. Hardwick*,
which held that the U.S. Constitution does not create a funda-

mental right to privacy which extends to homosexual acts. Lawrence and Garner appealed again, and in July 2002, the case arrived at the United States Supreme Court.

By a vote of 6-3, the Court struck down Texas's Homosexual Conduct law, overturned the men's convictions, and reversed the *Bowers* decision, which had the effect of invalidating sodomy laws throughout the nation. In his opinion for the majority, Justice Anthony Kennedy rejected the notion underpinning *Bowers*, that homosexual sodomy is a widely and historically condemned practice. That ruling, he said, "demeans the lives of homosexual persons." He declared that "the intimate, adult consensual conduct at issue here was part of the liberty protected by the substantive component of the Fourteenth Amendment's due process protections." In a passionate dissent, Justice Antonin Scalia accused the majority of legislating morality from the bench, pronouncing that the Court has "signed on to the so-called homosexual agenda."

Lawrence is considered one of the Court's more influential decisions with broad and far-reaching implications. The decision was hailed by the lesbian, gay, and transsexual community as an enormous legal victory because it changed the status of homosexual acts and emphasized that gays are entitled to full respect and equal claim to all constitutional rights. Although the case was decided on due process and not equal protection grounds, many groups have invoked the ruling to dispute other legal restrictions on homosexuality, including the right to state recognition of same-sex marriages.

> "When sexuality finds overt expression
> in intimate conduct with another per-
> son, the conduct can be but one ele-
> ment in a personal bond that is more
> enduring. The liberty protected by the
> Constitution allows homosexual per-
> sons the right to make this choice."

The Court's Decision: Criminalizing Sexual Intimacy by Same-Sex Couples Violates the Fourteenth Amendment

Anthony M. Kennedy

Anthony McLeod Kennedy was nominated by President Ronald Reagan to the Supreme Court in 1988. In his written opinion in Lawrence and Garner v. Texas, *Kennedy explains why the Court is striking down Texas sodomy laws and finding for the petitioners, John Geddes Lawrence and Tyron Garner, who had been charged with violating Texas's anti-sodomy statute, the Texas "Homosexual Conduct" law. In his opinion, Kennedy casts doubt on the findings of the Court in an earlier case,* Bowers v. Hardwick *(1982), which upheld a challenged Georgia statute and found no constitutional protection of sexual privacy. He also discounts the notion in the previous decision that history supported the ability of states to prohibit private, consensual homosexual activity. He argues that the intimate, adult consensual conduct at issue in the case was part of the liberty protected by the substantive component of the Fourteenth Amendment's due process*

Anthony M. Kennedy, John Geddes Lawrence and Tyron Garner, Petitioners v. Texas, *U.S. Supreme Court, June 26, 2003.*

protections; there is a fundamental right for consenting adults to engage in private sexual activity. He also points out that the Texas statute furthers no legitimate state interest that can justify its intrusion into the personal and private life of the individual. Bowers v. Hardwick, Kennedy concludes, should be overruled.

Liberty protects the person from unwarranted government intrusions into a dwelling or other private places. In our tradition the State is not omnipresent in the home. And there are other spheres of our lives and existence, outside the home, where the State should not be a dominant presence. Freedom extends beyond spatial bounds. Liberty presumes an autonomy of self that includes freedom of thought, belief, expression, and certain intimate conduct. The instant case involves liberty of the person both in its spatial and more transcendent dimensions.

Background to the Case

The question before the Court is the validity of a Texas statute making it a crime for two persons of the same sex to engage in certain intimate sexual conduct.

In Houston, Texas, officers of the Harris County Police Department were dispatched to a private residence in response to a reported weapons disturbance. They entered an apartment where one of the petitioners, John Geddes Lawrence, resided. The right of the police to enter does not seem to have been questioned. The officers observed Lawrence and another man, Tyron Garner, engaging in a sexual act. The two petitioners were arrested, held in custody over night, and charged and convicted before a Justice of the Peace.

The complaints described their crime as "deviate sexual intercourse, namely anal sex, with a member of the same sex (man)." The applicable state law is Tex. Penal Code Ann. §21.06(a) (2003). It provides: "A person commits an offense if he engages in deviate sexual intercourse with another individual of the same sex." The statute defines "[d]eviate sexual intercourse" as follows:

"(A) any contact between any part of the genitals of one person and the mouth or anus of another person; or

"(B) the penetration of the genitals or the anus of another person with an object."

The petitioners exercised their right to a trial *de novo*, ["over again"] in Harris County Criminal Court. They challenged the statute as a violation of the Equal Protection Clause of the Fourteenth Amendment and of a like provision of the Texas Constitution. Those contentions were rejected. The petitioners, having entered a plea of *nolo contendere* [a plea that subjects the defendant to punishment but pursuits denial of the alleged charges], were each fined $200 and assessed court costs of $141.25. . . .

Court of Appeals Rejects the Petitioners' Appeals

The Court of Appeals for the Texas Fourteenth District considered the petitioners' federal constitutional arguments under both the Equal Protection and Due Process Clauses of the Fourteenth Amendment. After hearing the case . . . the court, in a divided opinion, rejected the constitutional arguments and affirmed the convictions. . . . The majority opinion indicates that the Court of Appeals considered our decision in *Bowers v. Hardwick* (1986), to be controlling on the federal due process aspect of the case. *Bowers* then being authoritative, this was proper.

We granted certiorari [review] to consider three questions:

1. Whether Petitioners' criminal convictions under the Texas "Homosexual Conduct" law—which criminalizes sexual intimacy by same-sex couples, but not identical behavior by

different-sex couples—violate the Fourteenth Amendment guarantee of equal protection of laws?

2. Whether Petitioners' criminal convictions for adult consensual sexual intimacy in the home violate their vital interests in liberty and privacy protected by the Due Process Clause of the Fourteenth Amendment?

3. Whether *Bowers v. Hardwick* (1986) should be overruled?. . .

The petitioners were adults at the time of the alleged offense. Their conduct was in private and consensual.

Other Cases Involving Privacy and Liberty

We conclude the case should be resolved by determining whether the petitioners were free as adults to engage in the private conduct in the exercise of their liberty under the Due Process Clause of the Fourteenth Amendment to the Constitution. For this inquiry we deem it necessary to reconsider the Court's holding in *Bowers.*

There are broad statements of the substantive reach of liberty under the Due Process Clause in earlier cases, including *Pierce v. Society of Sisters* (1925), and *Meyer v. Nebraska* (1923); but the most pertinent beginning point is our decision in *Griswold v. Connecticut* (1965).

In *Griswold* the Court invalidated a state law prohibiting the use of drugs or devices of contraception and counseling or aiding and abetting the use of contraceptives. The Court described the protected interest as a right to privacy and placed emphasis on the marriage relation and the protected space of the marital bedroom.

After *Griswold* it was established that the right to make certain decisions regarding sexual conduct extends beyond the marital relationship. In *Eisenstadt v. Baird* (1972), the Court invalidated a law prohibiting the distribution of contraceptives to unmarried persons. The case was decided under the Equal

Protection Clause, but with respect to unmarried persons, the Court went on to state the fundamental proposition that the law impaired the exercise of their personal rights. . . .

Griswold and *Eisenstadt*

The opinions in *Griswold* and *Eisenstadt* were part of the background for the decision in *Roe v. Wade* (1973). As is well known, the case involved a challenge to the Texas law prohibiting abortions, but the laws of other States were affected as well. Although the Court held the woman's rights were not absolute, her right to elect an abortion did have real and substantial protection as an exercise of her liberty under the Due Process Clause. The Court cited cases that protect spatial freedom and cases that go well beyond it. *Roe* recognized the right of a woman to make certain fundamental decisions affecting her destiny and confirmed once more that the protection of liberty under the Due Process Clause has a substantive dimension of fundamental significance in defining the rights of the person. . . .

Bowers v. Hardwick

The facts in *Bowers* had some similarities to the instant case. A police officer, whose right to enter seems not to have been in question, observed Hardwick, in his own bedroom, engaging in intimate sexual conduct with another adult male. The conduct was in violation of a Georgia statute making it a criminal offense to engage in sodomy. One difference between the two cases is that the Georgia statute prohibited the conduct whether or not the participants were of the same sex, while the Texas statute, as we have seen, applies only to participants of the same sex. Hardwick was not prosecuted, but he brought an action in federal court to declare the state statute invalid. He alleged he was a practicing homosexual and that the criminal prohibition violated rights guaranteed to him by the Constitution. The Court, in an opinion by Justice

[Byron] White, sustained the Georgia law. Chief Justice [Warren] Burger and Justice [Lewis] Powell joined the opinion of the Court and filed separate, concurring opinions. Four Justices dissented.

The Court began its substantive discussion in *Bowers* as follows: "The issue presented is whether the Federal Constitution confers a fundamental right upon homosexuals to engage in sodomy and hence invalidates the laws of the many States that still make such conduct illegal and have done so for a very long time." That statement, we now conclude, discloses the Court's own failure to appreciate the extent of the liberty at stake. To say that the issue in *Bowers* was simply the right to engage in certain sexual conduct demeans the claim the individual put forward, just as it would demean a married couple were it to be said marriage is simply about the right to have sexual intercourse. The laws involved in *Bowers* and here are, to be sure, statutes that purport to do no more than prohibit a particular sexual act. Their penalties and purposes, though, have more far-reaching consequences, touching upon the most private human conduct, sexual behavior, and in the most private of places, the home. The statutes do seek to control a personal relationship that, whether or not entitled to formal recognition in the law, is within the liberty of persons to choose without being punished as criminals.

This, as a general rule, should counsel against attempts by the State, or a court, to define the meaning of the relationship or to set its boundaries absent injury to a person or abuse of an institution the law protects. It suffices for us to acknowledge that adults may choose to enter upon this relationship in the confines of their homes and their own private lives and still retain their dignity as free persons. When sexuality finds overt expression in intimate conduct with another person, the conduct can be but one element in a personal bond that is more enduring. The liberty protected by the Constitution allows homosexual persons the right to make this choice.

Having misapprehended the claim of liberty there presented to it, and thus stating the claim to be whether there is a fundamental right to engage in consensual sodomy, the *Bowers* Court said: "Proscriptions against that conduct have ancient roots." In academic writings, and in many of the scholarly *amicus* briefs filed to assist the Court in this case, there are fundamental criticisms of the historical premises relied upon by the majority and concurring opinions in *Bowers*. We need not enter this debate in the attempt to reach a definitive historical judgment, but the following considerations counsel against adopting the definitive conclusions upon which *Bowers* placed such reliance.

No Real History of Prohibitions Against Homosexuality

At the outset it should be noted that there is no longstanding history in this country of laws directed at homosexual conduct as a distinct matter. Beginning in colonial times there were prohibitions of sodomy derived from the English criminal laws passed in the first instance by the Reformation Parliament of 1533. The English prohibition was understood to include relations between men and women as well as relations between men and men. Nineteenth-century commentators similarly read American sodomy, buggery, and crime-against-nature statutes as criminalizing certain relations between men and women and between men and men. The absence of legal prohibitions focusing on homosexual conduct may be explained in part by noting that according to some scholars the concept of the homosexual as a distinct category of person did not emerge until the late 19th century.

[T]he historical grounds relied upon in *Bowers* are more complex than the majority opinion and the concurring opinion by Chief Justice Burger indicate. Their historical premises are not without doubt and, at the very least, are overstated.

It must be acknowledged, of course, that the Court in *Bowers* was making the broader point that for centuries there have been powerful voices to condemn homosexual conduct as immoral. The condemnation has been shaped by religious beliefs, conceptions of right and acceptable behavior, and respect for the traditional family. For many persons these are not trivial concerns but profound and deep convictions accepted as ethical and moral principles to which they aspire and which thus determine the course of their lives. These considerations do not answer the question before us, however. The issue is whether the majority may use the power of the State to enforce these views on the whole society through operation of the criminal law. "Our obligation is to define the liberty of all, not to mandate our own moral code."

Homosexuality and Recent History

In all events we think that our laws and traditions in the past half century are of most relevance here. These references show an emerging awareness that liberty gives substantial protection to adult persons in deciding how to conduct their private lives in matters pertaining to sex. "[H]istory and tradition are the starting point but not in all cases the ending point of the substantive due process inquiry."

This emerging recognition should have been apparent when *Bowers* was decided. In 1955 the American Law Institute promulgated the Model Penal Code and made clear that it did not recommend or provide for "criminal penalties for consensual sexual relations conducted in private." It justified its decision on three grounds: (1) The prohibitions undermined respect for the law by penalizing conduct many people engaged in; (2) the statutes regulated private conduct not harmful to others; and (3) the laws were arbitrarily enforced and thus invited the danger of blackmail. In 1961 Illinois changed its laws to conform to the Model Penal Code. Other States soon followed.

In *Bowers* the Court referred to the fact that before 1961 all 50 States had outlawed sodomy, and that at the time of the Court's decision 24 States and the District of Columbia had sodomy laws. Justice Powell pointed out that these prohibitions often were being ignored, however. Georgia, for instance, had not sought to enforce its law for decades.

The sweeping references by Chief Justice Burger to the history of Western civilization and to Judeo-Christian moral and ethical standards did not take account of other authorities pointing in an opposite direction. A committee advising the British Parliament recommended in 1957 repeal of laws punishing homosexual conduct. Parliament enacted the substance of those recommendations 10 years later.

Of even more importance, almost five years before *Bowers* was decided the European Court of Human Rights considered a case with parallels to *Bowers* and to today's case. An adult male resident in Northern Ireland alleged he was a practicing homosexual who desired to engage in consensual homosexual conduct. The laws of Northern Ireland forbade him that right. He alleged that he had been questioned, his home had been searched, and he feared criminal prosecution. The court held that the laws proscribing the conduct were invalid under the European Convention on Human Rights. Authoritative in all countries that are members of the Council of Europe (21 nations then, 45 nations now), the decision is at odds with the premise in *Bowers* that the claim put forward was insubstantial in our Western civilization.

Deficiencies in *Bowers*

In our own constitutional system the deficiencies in *Bowers* became even more apparent in the years following its announcement. The 25 States with laws prohibiting the relevant conduct referenced in the *Bowers* decision are reduced now to 13, of which 4 enforce their laws only against homosexual conduct. In those States where sodomy is still proscribed, whether for same-sex or heterosexual conduct, there is a pattern of nonenforcement with respect to consenting adults acting in private. The State of Texas admitted in 1994 that as of that date it had not prosecuted anyone under those circumstances.

Doubts Cast on *Bowers*

Two principal cases decided after *Bowers* cast its holding into even more doubt. In *Planned Parenthood of Southeastern Pa. v. Casey* (1992), the Court reaffirmed the substantive force of the liberty protected by the Due Process Clause. The *Casey* decision again confirmed that our laws and tradition afford constitutional protection to personal decisions relating to marriage, procreation, contraception, family relationships, child rearing, and education. . . .

Persons in a homosexual relationship may seek autonomy . . . just as heterosexual persons do. The decision in *Bowers* would deny them this right.

The second post-*Bowers* case of principal relevance is *Romer v. Evans* (1996). There the Court struck down class-based legislation directed at homosexuals as a violation of the Equal Protection Clause. *Romer* invalidated an amendment to Colorado's constitution which named as a solitary class persons who were homosexuals, lesbians, or bisexual either by "orientation, conduct, practices or relationships," and deprived them of protection under state antidiscrimination laws. We concluded that the provision was "born of animosity toward the class of persons affected" and further that it had no rational relation to a legitimate governmental purpose.

As an alternative argument in this case, counsel for the petitioners and some *amici* contend that *Romer* provides the basis for declaring the Texas statute invalid under the Equal Protection Clause. That is a tenable argument, but we conclude the instant case requires us to address whether *Bowers* itself has continuing validity. Were we to hold the statute invalid under the Equal Protection Clause some might question whether a prohibition would be valid if drawn differently, say, to prohibit the conduct both between same-sex and different-sex participants.

Equality of treatment and the due process right to demand respect for conduct protected by the substantive guarantee of liberty are linked in important respects, and a decision on the latter point advances both interests. If protected conduct is made criminal and the law which does so remains unexamined for its substantive validity, its stigma might remain even if it were not enforceable as drawn for equal protection reasons. When homosexual conduct is made criminal by the law of the State, that declaration in and of itself is an invitation to subject homosexual persons to discrimination both in the public and in the private spheres. The central holding of *Bowers* has been brought in question by this case, and it should be addressed. Its continuance as precedent demeans the lives of homosexual persons.

The stigma this criminal statute imposes, moreover, is not trivial. The offense, to be sure, is but a class C misdemeanor, a minor offense in the Texas legal system. Still, it remains a criminal offense with all that imports for the dignity of the persons charged. The petitioners will bear on their record the history of their criminal convictions. Just this Term we rejected various challenges to state laws requiring the registration of sex offenders. We are advised that if Texas convicted an adult for private, consensual homosexual conduct under the statute here in question the convicted person would come within the registration laws of a least four States were he or she to be subject to their jurisdiction. This underscores the consequential nature of the punishment and the state-sponsored condemnation attendant to the criminal prohibition. Furthermore, the Texas criminal conviction carries with it the other collateral consequences always following a conviction, such as notations on job application forms, to mention but one example. . . .

Bowers Overturned

The rationale of *Bowers* does not withstand careful analysis. In his dissenting opinion in *Bowers* Justice [John Paul] Stevens came to these conclusions:

> "Our prior cases make two propositions abundantly clear. First, the fact that the governing majority in a State has traditionally viewed a particular practice as immoral is not a sufficient reason for upholding a law prohibiting the practice; neither history nor tradition could save a law prohibiting miscegenation from constitutional attack. Second, individual decisions by married persons, concerning the intimacies of their physical relationship, even when not intended to produce offspring, are a form of "liberty" protected by the Due Process Clause of the Fourteenth Amendment. Moreover, this protection extends to intimate choices by unmarried as well as married persons."

Justice Stevens' analysis, in our view, should have been controlling in *Bowers* and should control here.

Bowers was not correct when it was decided, and it is not correct today. It ought not to remain binding precedent. *Bowers v. Hardwick* should be and now is overruled.

The present case does not involve minors. It does not involve persons who might be injured or coerced or who are situated in relationships where consent might not easily be refused. It does not involve public conduct or prostitution. It does not involve whether the government must give formal recognition to any relationship that homosexual persons seek to enter. The case does involve two adults who, with full and mutual consent from each other, engaged in sexual practices common to a homosexual lifestyle. The petitioners are entitled to respect for their private lives. The State cannot demean their existence or control their destiny by making their private sexual conduct a crime. Their right to liberty under the Due Process Clause gives them the full right to engage in their conduct without intervention of the government. "It is a promise of the Constitution that there is a realm of personal liberty which the government may not enter" [*Casey*]. The Texas statute furthers no legitimate state interest which can justify its intrusion into the personal and private life of the individual.

Had those who drew and ratified the Due Process Clauses of the Fifth Amendment or the Fourteenth Amendment known the components of liberty in its manifold possibilities, they might have been more specific. They did not presume to have this insight. They knew times can blind us to certain truths and later generations can see that laws once thought necessary and proper in fact serve only to oppress. As the Constitution endures, persons in every generation can invoke its principles in their own search for greater freedom.

"The Fourteenth Amendment expressly
allows States to deprive their citizens of
'liberty,' so long as 'due process of law'
is provided . . ."

Dissenting Opinion: The Majority Is Adopting the "Homosexual Agenda"

Antonin Scalia

*Antonin Gregory Scalia, nominated by President Ronald Reagan
to the Supreme Court, has served as an associate justice since
1986. Justice Scalia, joined by Chief Justice William Rehnquist
and Justice Clarence Thomas, dissented in the case of* Lawrence
and Garner v. Texas, *in which the Court found that Texas sodomy laws were unconstitutional. Scalia says that the Court was
not justified in overruling the precedent of* Bowers v. Hardwick,
*and argues that states should be able to make the moral judg-
ment that homosexual conduct is wrong and embody that judgment in criminal statutes. Scalia charges the Court as having
signed on to the "homosexual agenda" and fears that the
majority's analysis spelled the end of all morals-based regulation
of sexual conduct. Scalia further argues that* Lawrence *articu-
lates a standard for overturning precedent that, if consistently
applied, demands the overthrow of* Roe v. Wade. Lawrence, *he
explains, spells out a three-part test under which it would be appropriate to abandon precedent: when a previous decision's foundations have been eroded by subsequent decisions, when it has
been the subject of substantial and continuing criticism, and*

Antonin Scalia, *John Geddes Lawrence and Tyron Garner, Petitioners v. Texas*, U.S. Supreme Court, June 26, 2003.

when it has not induced individual or societal reliance that counsels against its reversal. Scalia believes that Roe meets the three conditions of this test.

"Liberty finds no refuge in a jurisprudence of doubt" [*Planned Parenthood of Southeastern Pa. v. Casey* (1992)]. That was the Court's sententious response, barely more than a decade ago, to those seeking to overrule *Roe v. Wade* (1973). The Court's response today, to those who have engaged in a 17-year crusade to overrule *Bowers v. Hardwick* (1986), is very different. The need for stability and certainty presents no barrier.

The Central Legal Conclusion of *Bowers* Untouched

Most of the rest of today's opinion has no relevance to its actual holding—that the Texas statute "furthers no legitimate state interest which can justify" its application to petitioners under rational-basis review. Though there is discussion of "fundamental proposition[s]," and "fundamental decisions," nowhere does the Court's opinion declare that homosexual sodomy is a "fundamental right" under the Due Process Clause; nor does it subject the Texas law to the standard of review that would be appropriate (strict scrutiny) if homosexual sodomy *were* a "fundamental right." Thus, while overruling the *outcome of Bowers*, the Court leaves strangely untouched its central legal conclusion: "[R]espondent would have us announce . . . a fundamental right to engage in homosexual sodomy. This we are quite unwilling to do." Instead the Court simply describes petitioners' conduct as "an exercise of their liberty"—which it undoubtedly is—and proceeds to apply an unheard-of form of rational-basis review that will have far-reaching implications beyond this case.

Overturning *Bowers*

I begin with the Court's surprising readiness to reconsider a decision rendered a mere 17 years ago in *Bowers v. Hardwick*. I do not myself believe in rigid adherence to *stare decisis* ["let the decision stand"] in constitutional cases; but I do believe that we should be consistent rather than manipulative in invoking the doctrine. Today's opinions in support of reversal do not bother to distinguish—or indeed, even bother to mention—the paean [declaration of praise] to *stare decisis* coauthored by three Members of today's majority in *Planned Parenthood v. Casey*. There, when *stare decisis* meant preservation of judicially invented abortion rights, the widespread criticism of *Roe* was strong reason to *reaffirm* it:

> "Where, in the performance of its judicial duties, the Court decides a case in such a way as to resolve the sort of intensely divisive controversy reflected in *Roe*[,] . . . its decision has a dimension that the resolution of the normal case does not carry. . . . [T]o overrule under fire in the absence of the most compelling reason . . . would subvert the Court's legitimacy beyond any serious questions." . . .

Should *Roe* and *Bowers* Both Be Overruled?

Today's approach to *stare decisis* invites us to overrule an erroneously decided precedent (including an "intensely divisive" decision) *if:* (1) its foundations have been "eroded" by subsequent decisions; (2) it has been subject to "substantial and continuing" criticism; and (3) it has not induced "individual or societal reliance" that counsels against overturning. The problem is that *Roe* itself—which today's majority surely has no disposition to overrule—satisfies these conditions to at least the same degree as *Bowers*.

(1) A preliminary digressive observation with regard to the first factor: The Court's claim that *Planned Parenthood v. Casey*, "casts some doubt" upon the holding in *Bowers* (or any other case, for that matter) does not withstand analysis. As far

as its holding is concerned, *Casey* provided a *less* expansive right to abortion than did *Roe, which was already on the books when Bowers was decided.* And if the Court is referring not to the holding of *Casey,* but to the dictum of its famed sweet-mystery-of-life passage ("'At the heart of liberty is the right to define one's own concept of existence, of meaning, of the universe, and of the mystery of human life'"): That "casts some doubt" upon either the totality of our jurisprudence or else (presumably the right answer) nothing at all. I have never heard of a law that attempted to restrict one's "right to define" certain concepts; and if the passage calls into question the government's power to regulate *actions based on* one's self-defined "concept of existence, etc.," it is the passage that ate the rule of law.

I do not quarrel with the Court's claim that *Romer v. Evans,* "eroded" the "foundations" of *Bowers'* rational-basis holding. But *Roe* and *Casey* have been equally "eroded" by *Washington v. Glucksberg* (1997), which held that *only* fundamental rights which are "'deeply rooted in this Nation's history and tradition'" qualify for anything other than rational basis scrutiny under the doctrine of "substantive due process." *Roe* and *Casey,* of course, subjected the restriction of abortion to heightened scrutiny without even attempting to establish that the freedom to abort *was* rooted in this Nation's tradition.

(2) *Bowers,* the Court says, has been subject to "substantial and continuing [criticism], disapproving of its reasoning in all respects, not just as to its historical assumptions." Exactly what those nonhistorical criticisms are, and whether the Court even agrees with them, are left unsaid, although the Court does cite two books. . . . Of course, *Roe* too (and by extension *Casey*) had been (and still is) subject to unrelenting criticism, including criticism from the two commentators cited by the Court today. . . .

(3) That leaves, to distinguish the rock-solid, unamendable disposition of *Roe* from the readily overrulable *Bowers*, only the third factor. "[T]here has been," the Court says, "no individual or societal reliance on *Bowers* of the sort that could counsel against overturning its holding. . . ." It seems to me that the "societal reliance" on the principles confirmed in *Bowers* and discarded today has been overwhelming. Countless judicial decisions and legislative enactments have relied on the ancient proposition that a governing majority's belief that certain sexual behavior is "immoral and unacceptable" constitutes a rational basis for regulation. . . .

Bowers as Precedent for Other Cases

We ourselves relied extensively on *Bowers* when we concluded, in *Barnes v. Glen Theatre, Inc.* (1991), that Indiana's public indecency statute furthered "a substantial government interest in protecting order and morality." State laws against bigamy, same-sex marriage, adult incest, prostitution, masturbation, adultery, fornication, bestiality, and obscenity are likewise sustainable only in light of *Bowers'* validation of laws based on moral choices. . . .

What a massive disruption of the current social order, therefore, the overruling of *Bowers* entails. . . .

To tell the truth, it does not surprise me, and should surprise no one, that the Court has chosen today to revise the standards of *stare decisis* set forth in *Casey*. It has thereby exposed *Casey's* extraordinary deference to precedent for the result-oriented expedient that it is.

Having decided that it need not adhere to *stare decisis*, the Court still must establish that *Bowers* was wrongly decided and that the Texas statute, as applied to petitioners, is unconstitutional.

There Are Constraints on Liberty

Texas Penal Code Ann. §21.06(a) (2003) undoubtedly imposes constraints on liberty. So do laws prohibiting prostitution, recreational use of heroin, and, for that matter, working more than 60 hours per week in a bakery. But there is no right to "liberty" under the Due Process Clause, though today's opinion repeatedly makes that claim. The Fourteenth Amendment *expressly allows* States to deprive their citizens of "liberty," *so long as "due process of law" is provided*:

> "No state shall . . . deprive any person of life, liberty, or property, *without due process of law*." (emphasis added).

Our opinions applying the doctrine known as "substantive due process" hold that the Due Process Clause prohibits States from infringing *fundamental* liberty interests, unless the infringement is narrowly tailored to serve a compelling state interest. We have held repeatedly, in cases the Court today does not overrule, that *only* fundamental rights qualify for this so-called "heightened scrutiny" protection—that is, rights which are "'deeply rooted in this Nation's history and tradition.'"

Bowers held, first, that criminal prohibitions of homosexual sodomy are not subject to heightened scrutiny because they do not implicate a "fundamental right" under the Due Process Clause. Noting that "[p]roscriptions against that conduct have ancient roots," that "[s]odomy was a criminal offense at common law and was forbidden by the laws of the original 13 States when they ratified the Bill of Rights," and that many States had retained their bans on sodomy, *Bowers* concluded that a right to engage in homosexual sodomy was not "'deeply rooted in this Nation's history and tradition.'"

The Court today does not overrule this holding. Not once does it describe homosexual sodomy as a "fundamental right" or a "fundamental liberty interest," nor does it subject the Texas statute to strict scrutiny. Instead, having failed to establish that the right to homosexual sodomy is "'deeply rooted in this Nation's history and tradition,'" the Court concludes that the application of Texas's statute to petitioners' conduct fails the rational-basis test, and overrules *Bowers*' holding to the contrary. . . .

What Is "Acting in Private"?

[T]he Court makes the claim, again unsupported by any citations, that "[l]aws prohibiting sodomy do not seem to have been enforced against consenting adults acting in private." The key qualifier here is "acting in private"—since the Court admits that sodomy laws *were* enforced against consenting adults (although the Court contends that prosecutions were "infrequent,"). I do not know what "acting in private" means; surely consensual sodomy, like heterosexual intercourse, is rarely performed on stage. If all the Court means by "acting in private" is "on private premises, with the doors closed and windows covered," it is entirely unsurprising that evidence of enforcement would be hard to come by. (Imagine the circumstances that would enable a search warrant to be obtained for a residence on the ground that there was probable cause to believe that consensual sodomy was then and there occurring.) Surely that lack of evidence would not sustain the proposition that consensual sodomy on private premises with the doors closed and windows covered was regarded as a "fundamental right," even though all other consensual sodomy was criminalized. There are 203 prosecutions for consensual, adult homosexual sodomy reported in the West Reporting system and official state reporters from the years 1880–1995. There are also records of 20 sodomy prosecutions and 4 executions during the colonial period. *Bowers'* conclusion that homosexual sodomy is not a fundamental right "deeply rooted in this Nation's history and tradition" is utterly unassailable.

Realizing that fact, the Court instead says: "[W]e think that our laws and traditions in the past half century are of most relevance here. These references show *an emerging awareness* that liberty gives substantial protection to adult persons in deciding how to conduct their private lives *in matters pertaining to sex.*" Apart from the fact that such an "emerging awareness" does not establish a "fundamental right," the statement is factually false. States continue to prosecute all sorts of crimes by adults "in matters pertaining to sex": prostitution, adult incest, adultery, obscenity and child pornography. . . .

Sexual Morality as a State's Interest

I turn now to the ground on which the Court squarely rests its holding: the contention that there is no rational basis for the law here under attack. This proposition is so out of accord with our jurisprudence—indeed, with the jurisprudence of *any* society we know—that it requires little discussion.

The Texas statute undeniably seeks to further the belief of its citizens that certain forms of sexual behavior are "immoral and unacceptable" the same interest furthered by criminal laws against fornication, bigamy, adultery, adult incest, bestiality, and obscenity. *Bowers* held that this *was* a legitimate state interest. The Court today reaches the opposite conclusion. The Texas statute, it says, "furthers *no legitimate state interest* which can justify its intrusion into the personal and private life of the individual." The Court embraces instead Justice Stevens' declaration in his *Bowers* dissent, that "the fact that the governing majority in a State has traditionally viewed a particular practice as immoral is not a sufficient reason for upholding a law prohibiting the practice." This effectively decrees the end of all morals legislation. If, as the Court asserts, the promotion of majoritarian sexual morality is not even a *legitimate* state interest, none of the above-mentioned laws can survive rational-basis review. . . .

The Court and the Homosexual Agenda

Today's opinion is the product of a Court, which is the product of a law-profession culture, that has largely signed on to the so-called homosexual agenda, by which I mean the agenda promoted by some homosexual activists directed at eliminating the moral opprobrium that has traditionally attached to homosexual conduct. I noted in an earlier opinion the fact that the American Association of Law Schools (to which any reputable law school *must* seek to belong) excludes from membership any school that refuses to ban from its job-interview facilities a law firm (no matter how small) that does not wish to hire as a prospective partner a person who openly engages in homosexual conduct.

One of the most revealing statements in today's opinion is the Court's grim warning that the criminalization of homosexual conduct is "an invitation to subject homosexual persons to discrimination both in the public and in the private spheres." It is clear from this that the Court has taken sides in the culture war, departing from its role of assuring, as neutral observer, that the democratic rules of engagement are observed. Many Americans do not want persons who openly engage in homosexual conduct as partners in their business, as scoutmasters for their children, as teachers in their children's schools, or as boarders in their home. They view this as protecting themselves and their families from a lifestyle that they believe to be immoral and destructive. The Court views it as "discrimination" which it is the function of our judgments to deter. So imbued is the Court with the law profession's anti-anti-homosexual culture, that it is seemingly unaware that the attitudes of that culture are not obviously "mainstream"; that in most States what the Court calls "discrimination" against those who engage in homosexual acts is perfectly legal; that proposals to ban such "discrimination" under Title VII have repeatedly been rejected by Congress; that in some cases such "discrimination" is *mandated* by federal statute; and that in some cases such "discrimination" is a constitutional right. . . .

Let me be clear that I have nothing against homosexuals, or any other group, promoting their agenda through normal democratic means. Social perceptions of sexual and other morality change over time, and every group has the right to persuade its fellow citizens that its view of such matters is the best. That homosexuals have achieved some success in that enterprise is attested to by the fact that Texas is one of the few remaining States that criminalize private, consensual homosexual acts. But persuading one's fellow citizens is one thing, and imposing one's views in absence of democratic majority will is something else. I would no more *require a* State to criminalize homosexual acts—or, for that matter, display *any* moral disapprobation of them—than I would *forbid* it to do so. What Texas has chosen to do is well within the range of traditional democratic action, and its hand should not be stayed through the invention of a brand-new "constitutional right" by a Court that is impatient of democratic change. It is indeed true that "later generations can see that laws once thought necessary and proper in fact serve only to oppress"; and when that happens, later generations can repeal those laws. But it is the premise of our system that those judgments are to be made by the people, and not imposed by a governing caste that knows best.

| "Lawrence *is potentially revolutionary not only because it abandons right to privacy in favor of liberty, but . . . [because] . . . there is not even the pretense of a 'fundamental right' rebutting the 'presumption of constitutionality.'"*

The Court Shifts Its Focus from Privacy to Liberty in the *Lawrence* Decision

Randy E. Barnett

Randy E. Barnett is the Carmack Waterhouse Professor of Legal Theory at the Georgetown University Law Center. In the follow-ing viewpoint, he explains why Lawrence and Garner v. Texas *could be a revolutionary case if the Supreme Court follows Jus-tice Kennedy's reasoning in the future. The Court found in* Lawrence *that the Texas sodomy statute under which the two petitioners, John Geddes Lawrence and Tyron Garner, were charged was unconstitutional. Kennedy, Barnett points out, finds the statute to be unconstitutional not because it infringes a right to privacy, but because it infringes "liberty"—something he men-tions more than two dozen times in his written opinion. In addi-tion, according to Barnett, Kennedy's opinion protects liberty without any finding that the liberty being restricted is a "funda-mental right." Instead, having identified the conduct prohibited as liberty, he turns to the purported justification for the statute and finds it inadequate. This represents a clear rejection of the*

Randy E. Barnett, "Justice Kennedy's Libertarian Revolution: *Lawrence v. Texas*," *Cato Supreme Court Review*, 2002–2003. Republished with permission of The Cato Institute, conveyed through Copyright Clearance Center, Inc.

"fundamental rights" jurisprudence as it has developed since Griswold v. Connecticut, *and the adoption of what appears to be a "presumption of liberty."*

I n *Lawrence [and Garner] v. Texas,* the Supreme Court held unconstitutional a Texas law criminalizing sexual relations between persons of the same sex. That would be reason enough to consider the case a landmark decision. But to those schooled in post-New Deal "fundamental rights" jurisprudence, what was most striking about *Lawrence* was the *way* the Court justified its ruling. If the approach the Court took in the case is followed in other cases in the future, we have in *Lawrence* nothing short of a constitutional revolution, with implications reaching far beyond the "personal liberty" at issue here.

Contrary to how their decision was widely reported, the *Lawrence* majority did not protect a "right of privacy." Instead, quite simply, they protected "liberty." Breaking free at last of the post-New Deal constitutional tension between the "presumption of constitutionality," on one hand, and "fundamental rights," on the other, Justice Anthony Kennedy and the four justices who joined his opinion did not begin by assuming the statute was constitutional. But neither did they call the liberty at issue "fundamental," which the modern Court would have been expected to do before withholding the presumption of constitutionality from the statute. Instead, the Court took the much simpler tack of requiring the state to justify its statute, whatever the status of the right at issue. . . .

Same-Sex Sexual Freedom

Lawrence is potentially revolutionary not only because it abandons a right to privacy in favor of liberty, but for another closely related reason: In the majority's opinion, there is not even the pretense of a "fundamental right" rebutting the "presumption of constitutionality." Justice Kennedy never mentions any presumption to be accorded the Texas statute.

More important, he never tries to justify the sexual liberty of same-sex couples as a fundamental right. Instead, he spends all of his energies demonstrating that same-sex sexual freedom is a legitimate aspect of liberty—unlike, for example, actions that violate the rights of others, which are not liberty but license. Not only does this take the Court outside the framework of Footnote Four [from *United States v. Carolene Products Company*, which introduced a more exacting standard of judicial review], it also removes it from the framework of unenumerated fundamental rights that was engrafted upon it in the wake of *Griswold* [*v. Connecticut*]. Until *Lawrence*, every unenumerated rights case had to establish that the liberty at issue was "fundamental," as opposed to a mere liberty interest.

Justice Scalia, in dissent, takes accurate note of all of this:

Though there is discussion of "fundamental proposition[s]," . . . and "fundamental decisions," . . . nowhere does the Court's opinion declare that homosexual sodomy is a "fundamental right" under the Due Process Clause; nor does it subject the Texas law to the standard of review that would be appropriate (strict scrutiny) if homosexual sodomy were a "fundamental right." Thus, while overruling the outcome of *Bowers*, the Court leaves strangely untouched its central legal conclusion: "[R]espondent would have us announce . . . a fundamental right to engage in homosexual sodomy. This we are quite unwilling to do." Instead the Court simply describes petitioners' conduct as "an exercise of their liberty"—which it undoubtedly is—and proceeds to apply an unheard-of form of rational-basis review that will have far-reaching implications beyond this case.

In other words, with liberty as the baseline, the majority places the onus on the government to justify its statutory restriction.

A "Presumption of Liberty"

Although he never acknowledges it, Justice Kennedy is employing here what I have called a "presumption of liberty" that requires the government to justify its restriction on liberty, instead of requiring the citizen to establish that the liberty being exercised is somehow "fundamental." In this way, once an action is deemed to be a proper exercise of liberty (as opposed to license), the burden shifts to the government.

All that was offered by the government to justify this statute is the judgment of the legislature that the prohibited conduct is "immoral," which for the majority (including, on this issue, Justice [Sandra Day] O'Connor) is simply not enough to justify the restriction of liberty. Why not? Here the Court is content to rest its conclusion on a quote from Justice Stevens's dissenting opinion in *Bowers*:

> Our prior cases make two propositions abundantly clear. First, the fact that the governing majority in a State has traditionally viewed a particular practice as immoral is not a sufficient reason for upholding a law prohibiting the practice; neither history nor tradition could save a law prohibiting miscegenation from constitutional attack. Second, individual decisions by married persons, concerning the intimacies of their physical relationship, even when not intended to produce offspring, are a form of "liberty" protected by the Due Process Clause of the Fourteenth Amendment. Moreover, this protection extends to intimate choices by unmarried as well as married persons."

A stronger defense of this conclusion is possible. A legislative judgment of "immorality" means simply that a majority of the legislature disapproves of this conduct. But justifying legislation solely on grounds of morality would entirely eliminate judicial review of legislative powers. How could a court ever adjudicate between a legislature's claim that a particular exercise of liberty is "immoral" and a defendant's contrary claim that it is not?

In practice, therefore, a doctrine allowing legislation to be justified solely on the basis of morality would recognize an unlimited police power in state legislatures. Unlimited power is the very definition of tyranny. Although the police power of states may be broad, it was never thought to be unlimited. . . .

In the end, *Lawrence* is a very simple, indeed elegant, ruling. Justice Kennedy examined the conduct at issue to see if it was properly an aspect of liberty (as opposed to license), and then asked the government to justify its restriction, which it failed to do adequately. The decision would have been far more transparent and compelling if Kennedy had acknowledged what was really happening (though perhaps that would have lost votes by other justices). Without that acknowledgment, the revolutionary aspect of his opinion is concealed and rendered vulnerable to the ridicule of the dissent. Far better would it have been to more closely track the superb amicus briefs of the Cato Institute, which Kennedy twice cited approvingly, and of the Institute for Justice.

Far-Reaching Implications

If the Court is serious in its ruling, Justice Scalia is right to contend that the shift from privacy to liberty, and away from the New Deal-induced tension between the presumption of constitutionality and fundamental rights, "will have far-reaching implications beyond this case." For example, the medical cannabis [marijuana] cases now wending their way through the Ninth Circuit would be greatly affected if those seeking to use or distribute medical cannabis pursuant to California law did not have to show that their liberty to do so was somehow "fundamental"—and instead the government were forced to justify its restrictions on that liberty. While wrongful behavior (or license) could be prohibited, rightful behavior (or liberty) could be regulated, provided that the regulation was shown to be necessary and proper.

Although it may be possible to cabin this case to the protection of "personal" liberties of an intimate nature—and it is a fair prediction that that is what the Court will attempt—for *Lawrence [and Garner] v. Texas* to be constitutionally revolutionary, the Court's defense of liberty must not be limited to sexual conduct. The more liberties the Court protects, the less ideological it will be and the more widespread political support it will enjoy. Recognizing a robust "presumption of liberty" might also enable the court to transcend the trench warfare over judicial appointments. Both Left and Right would then find their favored rights protected under the same doctrine. When the Court plays favorites with liberty, as it has since the New Deal, it loses rather than gains credibility with the public, and undermines its vital role as the guardian of the Constitution. If the Court is true to its reasoning, *Lawrence [and Garner] v. Texas* could provide an important step in the direction of a more balanced protection of liberty that could find broad ideological support.

> *"In declaring same-sex relationships entitled to respect,* Lawrence *also has advanced courts' views of the harms to couples denied the freedom to marry."*

Lawrence Bolsters the Case for Gay Marriage

David S. Buckel

David S. Buckel is senior counsel and the marriage project director for Lambda Legal, the oldest and largest national legal organization committed to achieving full recognition of the civil rights of lesbians, gay men, bisexuals, transgendered people, and people with HIV. In his article, Buckel comments on how the decision in Lawrence and Garner v. Texas, *which found a Texas sodomy statute to be unconstitutional, has advanced the case in American courts of the right of gay individuals to marry. He reviews a number of cases in different states in which the ban on marriage of same-sex couples has been struck down.* Lawrence, *he notes, has bolstered significant dissents to opinions that let stand bans on same-sex marriage as well. Buckel concludes that Lambda Legal will not relent in its use of the important case of* Lawrence *to defend the freedom of same-sex marriage.*

L ambda Legal's victory in *Lawrence [and Garner] v. Texas* torpedoed what was long ago christened the "gay exception" to the law, when courts abdicate their judicial role and impose personal or popular ideas of morality against the communities we serve. Nowhere is *Lawrence's* recognition of the judiciary's appropriate role more apparent than in our

David S. Buckel, "Building Marriage Equality with *Lawrence v. Texas*," *Of Counsel*, vol. 4, no. 3, May 29, 2008. Reproduced by permission.

cases seeking the freedom to marry. We saw it first surface in Massachusetts, and most recently in California. . . .

Other Cases Seeking Freedom to Marry

The Massachusetts Supreme Judicial Court struck down a ban on marriage for same-sex couples in a GLAD [Gay and Lesbian Advocates and Defenders] case, and relied on *Lawrence* to clarify the courts' important role in a democratic system of checks and balances among branches of government. First the court adopted *Lawrence*'s principle of judicial duty: "[o]ur obligation is to define the liberty of all, not to mandate our own moral code." Then the court affirmed its solemn role to defend a minority against the use of government power to discriminate: "the United States Supreme Court [in *Lawrence*] has reaffirmed that the Constitution prohibits a State from wielding its formidable power to regulate conduct in a manner that demeans basic human dignity, even though that statutory discrimination may enjoy broad public support."

With the vibrations still in the air, the Supreme Court of California just struck down a ban on marriage in our case litigated with lead counsel NCLR [National Center for Lesbian Rights] and the ACLU [American Civil Liberties Union]. That court relied on *Lawrence* at two significant junctures to maintain clarity for its judicial role in a democratic system of checks and balances. First, the court rejected the notion that courts define fundamental rights by virtue of who already enjoys the right. Second, quoting the axiom given life anew in *Lawrence*, the court rejected the notion that history and tradition can by themselves justify discrimination—"times can blind us to certain truths."

Similarly, in Lambda Legal's successful *Varnum v. Brien* case for marriage equality in Iowa, the trial judge struck down the state's marriage ban and in his opinion included several lengthy quotations from *Lawrence* on resisting the use of history and tradition to unhinge the court from its constitutional role. We're now on appeal working to preserve that solid opinion from the trial judge.

Harms of Denying Freedom to Marry

In declaring same-sex relationships entitled to respect, *Lawrence* also has advanced courts' views of the harms to couples denied the freedom to marry. In Massachusetts, the high court deployed *Lawrence* to explain that "[w]hether and whom to marry, how to express sexual intimacy, and whether and how to establish a family—these are among the most basic of every individual's liberty and due process rights." Notably, the Massachusetts court drew a more explicit link between *Lawrence* and the marriage bans in framing the proper constitutional analysis of those bans. The court observed that *Lawrence*, in striking down prohibitions on same-sex sexual intimacy, exposed the "punitive notions" of gay identity inherent in those prohibitions. Those punitive notions, along with other factors, "cemented the common and legal understanding of marriage as an unquestionably heterosexual institution." Thus *Lawrence* set the stage for the Massachusetts court's famous next line: "But it is circular reasoning, not analysis, to maintain that marriage must remain a heterosexual institution because that is what it historically has been."

We imported *Lawrence* to New Jersey as well. In Lambda Legal's successful *Lewis v. Harris* case, the New Jersey Supreme Court held that the legislature must, at minimum, provide the rights and responsibilities of marriage to same-sex couples (leaving for another day the question whether the powerful *name* of marriage is also required). Applying its unique balancing test, the court weighed the couples' interests against the state's interests and placed *Lawrence* itself on the scales. The court reasoned that along with other legal authority that raised expectations regarding gay people's interests in equality and liberty, *Lawrence* added concrete weight to same-sex couples' side of the scales.

"Good Dissents"

Despite our victories, no civil rights movement is a story of victory piling on top of victory, so while we litigate to win, we also prepare the foundation to "draw a good dissent," should the courts not live up to their role. *Lawrence* demonstrates the importance of that effort, concluding after heavy reliance on Justice [John Paul] Stevens' dissent in *Bowers v. Hardwick* (the earlier opinion that upheld Georgia's criminalization of sexual intimacy) that "Justice Stevens' analysis, in our view, should have been controlling in *Bowers* and should control here." Good dissents often become the law, as they have in other cases, including the dissents in cases like *Plessy v. Ferguson*, which preserved separate railroad coaches for African-Americans, *Lochner v. New York*, which overturned limits on workers' hours and *Hammer v. Dagenhart*, which struck down child labor laws. Well-reasoned dissents can shine a steady light on judicial failures to honor constitutional promises, a light not to be put out until the failure is put right.

Lawrence has bolstered significant dissents to opinions that let stand bans on marriage. Chief Judge Kaye of the New York Court of Appeals strongly dissented in that court's refusal to strike down a marriage ban. She observed that the *Lawrence* Court had warned against judicial reasoning that "misapprehends the nature of the liberty interest at stake." Then in the most forceful articulation yet of this point in case law, Chief Judge Kaye declared: "Simply put, fundamental rights are fundamental rights. They are not defined in terms of who is entitled to exercise them." Relying on another of Chief Judge Kaye's crisp statements, the Supreme Court of California rejected the idea that any harm befalls different-sex couples by allowing same-sex couples to marry, with this quotation from Chief Judge Kaye: "There are enough marriage licenses to go around for everyone."

The Maryland Court of Appeals also refused to strike down a marriage ban, and one dissent quoted extensively from Chief Judge Kaye's analysis:

"*Lawrence* rejected the notion that fundamental rights it had already identified could be restricted based on traditional assumptions about who should be permitted their protection. As the [*Lawrence*] Court noted, 'times can blind us to certain truths and later generations can see that laws once thought necessary and proper only serve to oppress.' As the Constitution endures, persons in every generation can invoke its principles in their own search for greater freedom."

That paragraph, which embodies thousands of hours of work by Lambda Legal and others, was written by a dissenting Maryland judge (in 2007) who was quoting Chief Judge Kaye (from 2006), who in turn was quoting *Lawrence* (2003) adopting Justice Stevens' dissent in *Bowers* (1986). Painful as the pace of change may be, this is often how our efforts as civil rights lawyers unfold, over time, ultimately fulfilling the promises of liberty and equality.

Another chief justice used *Lawrence* to moor her dissent in our New Jersey marriage case, agreeing with the majority's requirement that the legislature provide same-sex couples with all the rights and responsibilities of marriage, but declaring that the powerful word "marriage" was also necessary to honor the equality guarantee and that the court should not leave the matter for another day. Chief Justice Poritz cited the *Lawrence* Court's point about some laws serving only to oppress, and said the following of her court's refusal to carry out its constitutional duty in full: "Without analysis, our Court turns to history and tradition and finds that marriage has never been available to same-sex couples. That may be so—but the Court has not asked whether the limitation in our marriage laws, 'once thought necessary and proper in fact serve[s] only to oppress.'" Thus fortified by *Lawrence*, the Chief Justice addressed the possibility that the legislature might allow same-sex couples to marry one day, in a succinct statement later quoted by the Supreme Court of California: "That possibility does not relieve this Court of its responsibility to decide constitutional questions, no matter how difficult . . . The question of access to civil marriage by same-sex couples 'is not a matter of social policy but of constitutional interpretation.' It is a question for the Court to decide."

"Embarassments of History"

On the same theme of courts not abdicating their proper role, a dissenting intermediate appellate judge in the California marriage cases included an entire section in the opinion entitled "The Significance of *Lawrence v. Texas.*" Ultimately, based on *Lawrence*, the dissent concluded that "[j]udicial deference to the importance the state or many of its citizens attach to a traditional bias against homosexuals is fundamentally at war with judicial responsibility to protect the constitutional rights of traditionally disfavored minorities." That dissent was vindicated by our success on appeal to the Supreme Court of California.

Justices in other states have dissented more bluntly from the judicial rubber stamp of marriage bans. A Washington State high court justice cited *Lawrence* to emphasize the need for judges to "learn from the embarrassments of history," lessons ignored when the "plurality instead repeats the same transgressions." A second justice joined in that dissent, leaving no cover left on the honest truth:

> "Just as the United States Supreme Court majority did in *Bowers v. Hardwick* 20 years ago, [this Court] frame[s] the issue before us so as to ignore not only petitioners' fundamental right to privacy but also the legislature's blatant animosity toward gays and lesbians. . . . The passage of time and prudent judgment revealed the folly of *Bowers*, a mistake born of bigotry and flawed legal reasoning. . . . Alas, the same will be said of this court's decision today."

In defending the freedom to marry, as with our other important work, we will not relent in our use of *Lawrence* to educate courts about the embarrassments of legal history. Sometimes we win, sometimes we draw good dissents that later become law—that is the nature of civil rights work. But one day historians will trace the lines from Lambda Legal's victory in *Lawrence* to our own version of *Loving v. Virginia*, when the U.S. Supreme Court struck down the last of the bans on interracial marriage. We will say to that court what the NAACP [National Association for the Advancement of Colored People] Legal Defense and Education Fund recently said in its *amicus* brief to the California Supreme Court in support of us: "There is no reason for this Court to treat marriage between persons of the same sex any differently than it treated interracial marriages."

Organizations to Contact

The editors have compiled the following list of organizations concerned with the issues debated in this book. The descriptions are derived from materials provided by the organizations. All have publications or information available for interested readers. The list was compiled on the date of publication of the present volume; the information provided here may change. Be aware that many organizations take several weeks or longer to respond to inquiries, so allow as much time as possible.

American Civil Liberties Union (ACLU)
125 Broad Street, 18th Floor, New York, NY 10004
(212) 549-2500
e-mail: aclu@aclu.org
Web site: www.aclu.org

The American Civil Liberties Union (ACLU) works in courts, legislatures, and communities to defend and preserve the individual rights and liberties that the Constitution and laws of the United States guarantee everyone in the country. As part of its work, the ACLU issues reports that study and note developments in civil liberties.

Cato Institute
1000 Massachusetts Avenue NW
Washington, DC 20001-5403
(202) 842-0200
Web site: www.cato.org

The Cato Institute is a nonprofit public policy research foundation whose mission is to increase the understanding of public policies based on the principles of limited government, free markets, individual liberty, and peace. Every year, the institute commissions and publishes books and studies on a wide range of policy issues including taxing and spending, education, free speech, Social Security, regulation, federalism, individual rights, the rule of law, globalization, national security, and the environment.

Christian Coalition of America
PO Box 37030, Washington, DC   20013-7030
(202) 479-6900
Web site: www.cc.org

The Christian Coalition of America is the largest conservative grassroots political organization in the United States. The political organization states that it is made up of "pro-family" Americans who "care deeply about ensuring that the government serves to strengthen and preserve, rather than threaten, our families and our values." To that end, the coalition works to identify, educate, and mobilize Christians for effective political action. One of the issues on its legislative agenda is passing the Marriage Protection Amendment, the constitutional amendment banning same-sex marriage.

The Hemlock Society/Compassion and Choices
PO Box 101810, Denver, CO   80250-1810
(800) 247-7421
Web site: www.compassionandchoices.org

The nonprofit group The Hemlock Society, founded in 1980, provides information regarding options for dignified death and legalized physician aid in dying. The group is now partnered with the organization Compassion and Choices, which is active in legislatures and courts to reform laws that limit a patient's rights to end-of-life care and personal control.

Lambda Legal
120 Wall Street, New York, NY   10005-3904
(212) 809-8585
Web site: www.lambdalegal.org

Lambda Legal is a national organization committed to achieving full recognition of the civil rights of lesbians, gay men, bisexuals, transgender people, and those with HIV through impact litigation, education, and public policy work.

Leadership Conference on Civil Rights (LCCR)
1629 K Street NW, Washington, DC   20006
(202) 466-3311
Web site: www.civilrights.org

Leadership Conference on Civil Rights (LCCR), founded in 1950, is the nation's premier civil rights coalition, and has co-ordinated the national legislative campaign on behalf of every major civil rights law since 1957. LCCR consists of more than 192 national organizations, representing persons of color, women, children, labor unions, individuals with disabilities, older Americans, major religious groups, gays and lesbians, and civil liberties and human rights groups. Its mission is to promote the enactment and enforcement of effective civil rights legislation and policy.

Liberty Fund
8335 Allison Pointe Trail, Suite 300
Indianapolis, IN   46250-1684
(317) 842-0880
Web site: www.libertyfund.org

Liberty Fund is a private, educational foundation established to encourage the study of the ideal of a society of free and responsible individuals. The foundation develops, supervises, and finances its own educational activities to foster thought and encourage discourse on enduring issues pertaining to liberty.

People for the American Way
2000 M Street NW, Suite 400, Washington, DC   20036
(202) 467-4999
Web site: www.pfaw.org

Since 1981, People for the American Way has fought for equal rights, freedom of speech, religious liberty, and equal justice under the law for every American. The organization offers a variety of news and reports on its Web site.

For Further Research

Books

Alice Fleetwood Bartee, *Privacy Rights: Cases Lost and Causes Won Before the Supreme Court*. Lanham, MD: Rowman & Littlefield Publishers, Inc. 2006.

Linda Colley, *Taking Stock of Taking Liberties: A Personal View*. London: British Library, 2009.

Michael Kent Curtis, *No State Shall Abridge: The Fourteenth Amendment and the Bill of Rights*. Durham, NC: Duke University Press, 1990.

Garrett Epps, *Democracy Reborn: The Fourteenth Amendment and the Fight for Equal Rights in Post-Civil War America*. New York: Holt Paperbacks, 2007.

Lee Epstein, *Constitutional Law for a Changing America: Rights, Liberties, and Justice*. Washington, DC: CQ Press, 2006.

Amitai Etzioni, *The Limits of Privacy*. New York: Basic Books, 2000.

Elizabeth Price Foley, *Liberty for All: Reclaiming Individual Privacy in a New Era of Public Morality*. New Haven, CT: Yale University Press, 2006.

John W. Johnson, *Griswold v. Connecticut: Birth Control and the Constitutional Right of Privacy*. Lawrence, KS: University Press of Kansas, 2005.

Ken I. Kersch, *Constructing Civil Liberties: Discontinuities in the Development of American Constitutional Law*. Cambridge, MA: Cambridge University Press, 2004.

Edward Keynes, *Liberty, Property, and Privacy: Toward a Jurisprudence of Substantive Due Process*. University Park, PA: Pennsylvania State University Press, 1996.

Darien A. McWhirter and Jon D. Bible, *Privacy as a Constitutional Right: Sex, Drugs, and the Right to Life*. Westport, CT: Quorum Books, 1992.

Rachel F. Moran, *Interracial Intimacy: The Regulation of Race and Romance*. Chicago, IL: University of Chicago Press, 2001.

National Archives and Records Administration, *The Bill of Rights: Evolution of Personal Liberties*. Santa Barbara, CA: ABC/CLIO, 2001.

William Nelson, *The Fourteenth Amendment: From Political Principle to Judicial Doctrine*. Cambridge, MA: Harvard University, 1998.

John W. Orth, *Due Process of Law: A Brief History*. Lawrence, KS: University Press of Kansas, 2003.

David A.J. Richards, *The Sodomy Cases: Bowers v. Hardwick and Lawrence v. Texas*. Lawrence, KS: University Press of Kansas, 2009.

Glenn E. Tinder, *Liberty: Rethinking an Imperiled Ideal*. Grand Rapids, MI: Willam B. Eerdmans Publishing, 2007.

Peter Wallenstein, *Tell the Court I Love My Wife: Race, Marriage, and Law—An American History*. New York: Palgrave Macmillan, 2004.

Marilyn Webb, et al., *The Good Death: The New American Search to Reshape the End of Life*. New York: Bantam Books, 1997.

William M. Wiecek, *Liberty Under Law: The Supreme Court in American Life*. Baltimore, MD: The Johns Hopkins University Press, 1988.

Sue Woodman, *Last Rights: The Struggle over the Right to Die*. New York: Plenum Press, 1998.

Periodicals

General

Martha Albertson Fineman, "Intimacy Outside of The Natural Family: The Limits Of Privacy," *Connecticut Law Review*, vol. 23, no. 4, Summer 1991, pp. 955–999.

Marouf Hasian Jr., "Vernacular Legal Discourse: Revisiting the Public Acceptance of the 'Right to Privacy' in the 1960s," *Political Communication*, vol. 18, no. 1, January–March 2001, pp. 89–106.

David A. Lewis, "The Fourteenth Amendment Through *Roe*-Colored Glasses: Unenumerated Rights and the 'Imperial Judiciary,'" *Polity*, vol. 39, no. 1, January 2007, pp. 103–25.

National Journal, "Problems with 'Privacy' and What to Do About *Roe*," vol. 37, no. 40, October 1, 2005, pp. 2991–92.

Women's Rights Law Reporter, "Substantive Due Process Comes Home to Roost: Fundamental Rights, *Griswold* to *Bowers*," vol. 10, nos. 2–3, Winter 1988, pp. 177–208.

Griswold v. Connecticut

Alan Freeman and Elizabeth Mensch, "The Court & the Sexual Revolution," *Commonweal*, vol. 121, no. 18, October 21, 1994, pp. 19–24.

David Glenn, "Looking Back at a Landmark Court Decision in the Formal Development of a Right of Privacy," *The Chronicle of Higher Education*, vol. 51, no. 40, June 10, 2005.

Thomas Halper, "Privacy and Autonomy: From Warren and Brandeis to *Roe* and *Cruzan*," *The Journal of Medicine and Philosophy*, vol. 21., no. 2, April 1996.

David Helscher, *"Griswold v. Connecticut* and the Unenumerated Right of Privacy," *Northern Illinois University Law Review*, vol. 15, no. 33, 1994, pp. 1–7.

Bradley P. Jacob, *"Griswold* and the Defense of Traditional Marriage," *North Dakota Law Review*, vol. 83, no. 4, Fall 2007, pp. 1199–1225.

Laura Kalman, "Review: The Promise and Peril of Privacy," *Reviews in American History*, vol. 22, no. 4, 1994, pp. 725–731.

Andrea Lockhart, *"Griswold v. Connecticut*: A Case Brief," *Journal of Contemporary Legal Issues*, vol. 14, no. 35, 1997, pp. 1–3.

Anthony Musante, "Black and White: What Law and Literature Can Tell Us About the Disparate Opinions in *Griswold v. Connecticut*," *Oregon Law Review*, vol. 85, no. 3, Fall 2006, pp. 853–894.

Loving v. Virginia

Alfred P. Doblin, "Loving Legacy for Full Marriage Equality," *The Record*, May 12, 2008, p. A11.

Brent Staples, *"Loving v. Virginia* and the Secret History of Race," *New York Times*, vol. 157, no. 54310, May 14, 2008, A22(L).

Washington v. Glucksberg

John Dinan, "Rights and the Political Process: Physician-Assisted Suicide in the Aftermath of *Washington v. Glucksberg*," *Publius*, vol. 31, no. 4, Fall 2001.

Lawrence O. Gostin, "Deciding Life and Death in the Courtroom: From *Quinlan* to *Cruzan, Glucksberg*, and *Vacco*—A Brief History and Analysis of Constitutional Protection of the 'Right to Die,'" *Journal of the American Medical Association*, vol. 278, no. 18, November 12, 1997.

————, "Liberty Interest in Aided Suicide Rejected; Court Finds No Constitutionally Protected Interest, Distinguishes the Withdrawal of Life Support," *The National Law Journal*, vol. 19, no. 50, August 11, 1997.

Alexa Hansen, "Unqualified Interests, Definitive Definitions: *Washington v. Glucksberg* and the Definition of Life," *Hastings Constitutional Law Quarterly*, vol. 36, no. 1, Fall 2008.

Yale Kamisar, "Can *Glucksberg* Survive *Lawrence?* Another Look at the End of Life and Personal Autonomy," *Michigan Law Review*, vol. 106, no. 8, June 2008.

John Keown, "No Constitutional Right to Physician-Assisted Suicide?" *Cambridge Law Journal*, vol. 56, no. 3, November 1997, pp. 506–509.

Martha Minow, "Which Question? Which Lie? Reflections on the Physician-Assisted Suicide Cases," *Supreme Court Review*, Annual 1997, pp. 1–30.

Lawrence and Garner v. Texas

Howard J. Bashman, "*Lawrence* Fails to Open Sexual Freedom Floodgates," *Texas Lawyer*, March 12, 2007.

Russell Blackford, "*Lawrence v. Texas*: A Right to Personal Freedom?" *Quadrant*, vol. 47, no. 11, November 2003, pp. 34–42.

Joel Brinkley, "Supreme Court Strikes Down Texas Law Banning Sodomy," *New York Times*, June 26, 2003.

Marcia Coyle, "Due Process," *Miami Daily Business Review*, December 26, 2003.

Thomas R. Eddlem, "Homogenizing Homosexuality: Using Techniques That Allow a Tiny Minority to Gain Power over a Complacent Majority, Homosexual Activists Are Leading Massachusetts (and America) Down into a Moral Abyss," *The New American*, November 28, 2005.

Richard Kim, "Queer Cheer," *The Nation*, vol. 277, no. 3, July 21, 2003.

Joseph Landau, "Misjudged—What *Lawrence* Hasn't Wrought," *The New Republic*, February 16, 2004.

Charles Lane, "Supreme Court Strikes Down Texas Sodomy Law," *Washington Post*, June 26, 2003.

The Recorder, "Five Years Later: The Lasting Effects of '*Lawrence*,'" June 27, 2008.

Warren Richey and Linda Feldmann, "Big Boost for Privacy Rights," *Christian Science Monitor*, June 26, 2003.

Laurence H. Tribe, "*Lawrence v. Texas*: The 'Fundamental Right' That Dare Not Speak Its Name," *Harvard Law Review*, vol. 117, 2004.

Camille Williams, "Why the Law Should Discourage Some Sexual Practices," *World and I*, vol. 19, no. 6, June 2004.

Index

A

Abigail Roberson v. Rochester Folding Box Co. (1902), 39
Abortion, 15, 50, 55–60, 131–133, 144–149
  See also *Planned Parenthood v. Casey* (1992); Reproductive rights; *Roe v. Wade* (1973)
ACLU (American Civil Liberties Union), 62, 98–99, 163, 186
Alabama, NAACP v. (1958), 24, 26
Alabama, Pace v. (1883), 71, 79
Alito, Samuel A., Jr., 56–57
Allied Stores of Ohio, Inc. v. Bowers (1959), 70
American Association of Law Schools, 176–177
American Civil Liberties Union. *See* ACLU (American Civil Liberties Union)
American Medical Association, 125
Andersen v. Kings County (2006), 111
Aptheker v. Secretary of State (1964), 38
Ashcroft, Planned Parenthood Federation of America v. (2004), 58
Assisted suicide
  Due Process Clause and, 115–116, 118, 121–124, 124, 129–131, 140–142
  mental competency and, 137–138, 141

personal autonomy and, 139–143, 146, 147
  religion and, 136, 138
  states' assisted-suicide bans, 118–120
  states' powers, 150–152
  See also *Glucksberg, Washington v.* (1997)
Autonomy of self
  assisted suicide, 139–143, 146, 147
  liberty and, 157

B

Baehr v. Lewin (1993), 109–110
Baird, Eisenstadt v. (1972), 48, 50, 120, 159–160
Baker v. State (1999), 110–112
Barnes v. Glen Theatre, Inc. (1991), 173
Barnett, Randy E., 179–184
Barnette, West Virginia State Board of Education v. (1943), 130
Barnum, P.T., 17
Barrows v. Jackson (1953), 22
Bazile, Leon, 63
Bell, Buck v. (1927), 82
Bill of Rights
  Fifth Amendment, 18, 32
  First Amendment, 17–18, 23–24, 28–29, 34, 35–36
  Fourth Amendment, 18, 29, 30, 32
  Ninth Amendment, 17–18, 32, 42
  penumbras, 18, 20–21, 23–25, 41–42, 45